Easy Peasy Vegan Eats

Healthy Cooking for Busy Peeps

MARY LAWRENCE

To every person who makes a difference
by shining their light on the world,
standing up for the voiceless, and refusing to
give in or give up, with all of my heart
I thank you. You are brave heroes.

Published by Well on Wheels, New Haven, CT.
www.wellonwheels.com
http://wellonwheels.blogspot.com

 wellonwheelsllc   wellonwheels

All products mentioned in this book are trademarks of their respective companies.
No claims of endorsement are made by including these products.
Printed in the United States of America.
First edition, paperback.

Layout design by Koloa Designs, Paramaribo, Suriname S.A.

Acknowledgements

Many of us lead busy, stressful lives and we often neglect to take the time to just sit and breathe quietly, slowly. It is no wonder that we also see mealtime as a stressful event, an added chore rather than a simple pleasure to savor at the end of the day.

I am grateful to those of you who have come to my cooking classes and requested recipes that are quick and easy to make, yet also satisfying. This is a theme that resonated fully with me, and so I wanted to share with you recipes that appeal to the senses, are as healthful as they are delicious, yet are uncomplicated enough to encourage you to experiment in the kitchen. Whether you're a new vegan or simply a home chef looking for healthy recipes that aren't a headache to prepare, consider this cookbook a guide to a simpler life.

I am also grateful to my clients who have entrusted in me the task of preparing their weekly meals. It has been an honor to create nourishing food in your kitchens and a joy to receive your enthusiastic response. I'm happy to be able to make healthy eating easier for all of you.

There are numerous others I wish to thank for their support and inspiration in bringing this cookbook to fruition. Your continued encouragement has made all the difference in keeping me motivated and determined to accomplish this goal. My enthusiastic recipe testers: Linda Campanelli, Nancy Cashman, Tamera Edwards, Jessica Greenebaum, Rosemary Lachance, Devin Pray and Danielle Petrovich for your exquisite taste, meticulous attention to detail, timely response and helpful critiques of my recipes. You reigned in the complexity to ensure these would be easy peasy to prepare for any skill level. To my manuscript reviewers: Jessica Greenebaum, George Lenker, Dr. Joel Marks, Alex Pierpaoli, Devin Pray, Caitlin Sorge, and Eric Triffin, thank you for your editorial direction, helpful suggestions, provocative questions, and gentle tweaking of tone and content. To Gary Kaplan for his expertise and assistance in getting me through my first attempt at layout design. To Joshua Fernandes (Koloa Designs) for making my vision a reality. To some of my mentors, Ken Bergeron for his finesse with vegan food, Mark Shadle for letting me get my feet wet in his restaurant, Dr. H. Robert Silverstein my doctor who supported my vegan transition, Dr. Nancy White for opening my eyes to naturopathy, the brilliant historian Rynn Berry who inspired me to write recipes and learn the history of vegetarianism, vegan nutrition experts Dr. Michael Greger, Dr. T. Colin Campbell, Dr. Caldwell Esselstyn, Dr. Neil Barnard, Dr. Milton Mills, and so many others who I've learned from.

To the vegan community—both local and virtual—which is too vast to thank individually as it is happily growing every day, you are always there for me when I need your support and encouragement the most. Thank you for fighting the good fight, for being a voice for the animals, and for never giving up or giving in until the day they are all free.

To my friends who have stuck with me through the years and who know that being vegan is part of who I am. Thank you for understanding and for caring about animals. I'm glad to have you along on the vegan journey. Maribeth Abrams, Tracy Albernaz, Nicholas Anthis (Georgie's & Shoreline Diner), Stacy Attenburg (Feral Cat Lady Supreme), Dianna Baros (and Camden, Bash & Bax), Dawn Barson, Carol Belau & Michael Kot, Tracy Benedict, Susan Bennett, Lisa Bonaldi (and Lily), Allan Brison, Jennifer Brosious,

Julia Caruk, Joan Casella Fellinger, Mona Cavallero, Jerry Cook, April D'Amato, Peter Dodge (and the Edge crew), Alaina Driscoll, Joshua Forgotson, Anne Garland, John Gatto, Lola Goldberg, Joyce & Harry Greenberg, Karen Gregaitis, Ironwoman Ruth Heidrich, Allie Holaday & Ted Rice, Annie & Neil Hornish, Karen James, Nicole Jamieson, Gary Kaplan, Leslie Kerz, Barbara King, Bun Lai (best vegan sushi), Steve LaPenta (The Bridge Man), Karen Laski, Gina Ledwith, Corinne Levin-Wozniewski, Glaucia Lolli, Steve MacLaughlin, Lauri MacLean, Alyssa Marchese, Rohit Kumar Mehta, Mark Minotti (Musical Forest), Doug Moss, Martha Moss, April Gallant Murasky (and Mr. Jonesy), Judy Panciera, Christina Pirello (my inspiration!), Cathy Popp, Angie Pugliese, Nancy Rice, Robin Robertson, Jeff Rosenberg, Debbi Roy, Kathleen Schurman (piggies!), Sandi Kahn Shelton, Gina Sinese, Sami Sunchild (your light will always shine), Hillary Thompkins, Maria Tupper, Paul Valdes, Jr., Liz Vitale, Joshua Warchol & Tracy Lake, Diane Wagemann (and Divine Treasures), Eileen & Jay Walker, Bonnie West, Natalie Westbrook.

An extra special thank you goes to my parents, Joe and Fran Lawrence, who have supported me through this entire adventure. Although they were skeptical when I first became vegan and questioned my sanity when I decided to pursue this as my livelihood, once they realized my passion and dedication, they joined in wholeheartedly. I also thank my brother, Joe, for cheering on his crazy little sister during difficult times, and for caring about animals, especially my two best friends, Lily and Zinnia. Carry on, Gremlin and Boo Bear.

I am honored to know all of you, and I thank you for being a part of my life. Your enthusiasm has been my inspiration.

No matter how busy things get, always remember to take the time to be mindful of the food you eat. The most important ingredient to any successful meal is that it is prepared with love, for that alone will make all the difference. I hope you enjoy these recipes as much as I do, and that they inspire you to share delicious vegan food with those you care about.

Go vegan... for you, the animals, and the planet.

Dedication

To my best friend and inspiration, who tested my patience, challenged my sanity, and taught me that love is about understanding and acceptance, I dedicate this book to your memory. Every day was an adventure with you. We climbed mountains together, camped in the woods, swam and ran, charged up hills, bunny-hopped through the snow, jumped in leaves, crab-dogged in the sand, and played tug of war and fetch with sticks and ropes and blankets and the noisiest squeaky toys we could find. Even during the most difficult times, you reminded me that the only thing that matters is to have fun, and if I ever forgot, you swatted me in the face. I miss you every day, but I'm forever grateful for what you gave me. Thank you for the courage to forge ahead when it felt pointless to continue. There's only so much one person can do, but you made me believe I could do anything.

Zinnia (Zinny, Baby Binz)

You're always in my heart.

"You must be imaginative, strong-hearted. You must try things that may not work, and you must not let anyone define your limits because of where you come from. Your only limit is your soul.

~ Chef Gusteau, *Ratatouille*

Introduction

When I started my vegan personal chef business back in 2003, I had no idea it would grow to become self-supportive professionally. I only knew that I loved cooking healthy vegan food and sharing it with people I cared about. It was an inauspicious beginning; I had a background in education and cooking was my passion, so I decided to combine the two and teach adult education cooking classes. The feedback was unanimously positive, with students begging me to open a restaurant or catering service because they couldn't wait to come back for more. When one of my students asked, "Will you come to my house and cook for me?" I thought she was joking. She wasn't. Instead, she became my first customer.

From that humble beginning, I was referred to a friend of hers who quickly became another customer, and through word of mouth I developed enough of a clientele that I was able to quit my day job. In just three years I had transformed a part-time hobby that I did simply for fun and a little extra income into a full-time business. I now have a steady customer base of weekly clients, offer private cooking and raw food lessons, teach classes, give lectures and cooking demonstrations, and consult with restaurants looking for healthy vegan recipes to add to their menu.

Over the years of cooking in so many clients' homes, I've developed techniques that have helped me become more efficient in any kitchen. Whether it's a tiny galley condo kitchen, a luxurious state of the art kitchen with 8-burner gas stove and all the bells and whistles, or even a portable butane burner set up on a picnic table, the process is always the same. Each time I cook it's like orchestrating a musical production, with every ingredient seamlessly coming together into a symphony of tastes, colors, and textures, pleasing to all of the senses. I envision the end result and know how to get there while staying calm, focused, and organized. There is a process I follow every time I cook which serves as my roadmap. These are the "easy peasy" techniques I hope to share with you in this book.

I'm often asked how I manage to cook a week's worth of meals in just a few hours, especially when it's in a stranger's kitchen. The answer is simple: by being fast, smart, and efficient. This is a talent I've developed over the years through hours of practice, trial and error, patience, and even a little sweat and tears (which no one sees when you're cooking alone!). Fortunately, I've made all the mistakes myself so you don't have to, and instead you can just reap the benefits.

In this cookbook, I offer my toolbox of tried and true kitchen techniques that I use on a daily basis whether cooking for myself, busy professionals, a finicky family, or a boisterous party. It's what has worked for me over the many years of running my successful business as a personal chef, and it can work for you in your kitchen, too. Whether you're an overwhelmed newbie vegan or an experienced chef who wants to tame the frazzle, these tips will help you save time, money, and your sanity. You will be astounded at how easy peasy vegan cooking can be.

Eat well, live well, be well!

Chapter 1

I Feel Good

We all have a story that leads us to that vegan fork in the road. For me, it was health issues that started me on this path. I was tired all the time and had seasonal allergies, asthma, a chronic cough, acne, headaches, and frequent bouts of sinusitis that left me breathless and believing I'd be carrying around an oxygen tank in a shopping cart for the rest of my life. It was on the precipice of my thirtieth birthday that I decided I didn't want to live this way any more.

Traditional allergists gave me two directives: get rid of my dog and take steroids for the rest of my life. Because I was skeptical of anyone who would suggest I part with a family member and I didn't want to be a slave to the pharmaceutical industry, I decided to seek other treatment options. This began my journey learning about alternative medicine, herbal therapy, and how food can affect one's health. My life, and my health, completely turned around as a result. It seems so obvious to me now, but it was all new 17 years ago, and for many of you reading this, it may still be.

There were many other attempts to move in the vegan direction prior to this crossroads, yet somehow I never felt quite "ready." In college I had tried, and failed (miserably), to become vegan when a friend introduced me to The Smiths' "Meat Is Murder" album. I couldn't help but make the intellectual connection, though my palate wasn't able to make the transition away from pizza and nachos at the time. As a child I had always loved animals and instinctively knew there was something unsettling about the hunk of steak on my plate oozing with "juice." When I would go fishing with my dad, I became horrified one day when I suddenly realized that the fish I was pulling off the hook was struggling for its last breath all because of me. There were many flies swatted and spiders squashed that left me feeling pangs of remorse. Even as a six-year-old, that connection was painfully palpable. Those experiences have stuck with me, and somehow, I always knew this was my destiny. But I needed some questions answered first.

Vegan 101

Having finally made the decision to abandon my culinary heritage and become vegan, the initial concern that I immediately needed to address was how could I possibly be healthy if I didn't eat meat, eggs, and dairy? While this may be a nagging question for many at first, let me reassure you that it need not be of concern as long as you eat a varied, whole-foods, plant-based diet emphasizing fresh fruits and vegetables. Making the recipes in this cookbook is an easy way to do so.

While I'm not a medical professional, my recommendations are based on years of nutrition research culminating in obtaining a certificate in plant-based nutrition from the T. Colin Campbell Foundation at eCornell, and applying sound dietary guidelines that work best for me. At the foundation are the core principles of vegan nutrition espoused by medical experts such as Dr. Milton Mills, Dr. Caldwell Esselstyn, Dr. T. Colin Campbell, and Dr. Michael Greger (http://nutritionfacts.org), as well as vegan RDs Ginny Kisch Messina (www.TheVeganRD.com),

Brenda Davis (http://brendadavisrd.com), Julieanna Hever (www.PlantBasedDietician.com), and Jack Norris (http://jacknorrisrd.com). All advocate eating whole plant-based foods in their natural state, preferably organic, emphasizing fresh fruits and vegetables that boost the immune system, aid in digestion, and prevent and reverse disease. The synergistic effect of these foods keeps the body strong, energized, and in balance. While there isn't one nutrient that should be isolated above all others, for vegans who are making the transition, paying attention to those perceived as most essential when eliminating animal products from your diet will help you become a confident, health-conscious vegan.

• **Complete Proteins.** These contain all 9 of the essential amino acids that the body can't produce. Protein helps build and repair cells and muscles. The RDA recommends we take in about 0.36 grams of protein per pound that we weigh, so we don't need much to be healthy. Conversely, too much protein (particularly from animal products) can cause the body to become acidic and prone to disease. Also keep in mind that ALL plant-based food contain protein, and there is no need for meticulous combining of various types. Sources: hemp seed, soy, quinoa, spirulina, amaranth, buckwheat

• **Calcium.** This is an essential mineral that not only makes bones strong, but also helps regulate blood pressure and keep weight under control. When I learned that figs and almonds contain substantial amounts of calcium, I made them my daily snack routine. Sources: cruciferous vegetables (broccoli, cauliflower, Brussels Sprouts), leafy greens (kale, collard, turnip greens), tofu, sesame seeds (and tahini), navy beans, chickpeas, blackstrap molasses, figs, almonds

• **Iron.** Iron helps carry oxygen in our blood through our bodies. To increase iron absorption and prevent iron deficiency, eat with a food containing vitamin C. Sources: dried fruits (prunes, raisins, apricots), dried beans and lentils, whole grains, leafy greens (spinach, kale, chard, collard), tofu, tempeh

• **Omega-3 Fat.** Omega-3 fatty acids (DHA, AHA, EPA) help reduce inflammation, lower cholesterol, lower blood pressure, and increase immune function. Sources: flax seeds, hemp seeds, chia seeds, walnuts, soy beans, microalgae

• **Vitamin B12.** B12 helps the brain and nervous system function and is a key component of hemoglobin which carries oxygen to cells through the blood. This is about the only nutrient vegans should be concerned about getting in supplement form. While you don't need much, long-term deficiency can lead to permanent nerve damage. The best absorbed form is sublingual methylcobalamin at a dose of 25-100 micrograms per day.

• **Antioxidants.** Vitamins C, A, and E are found in abundance in plant-based foods. They boost the immune system, protect cells from free radical damage, and increase absorption of iron. Sources: Tropical fruits (papaya, cantaloupe, pineapple), citrus fruits (oranges, lemons, limes), berries (strawberries, raspberries, blueberries, cranberries), greens (kale, collard, spinach), cruciferous vegetables (broccoli, Brussels sprouts, cabbage)

A Word about Diet

Often people choose a whole foods plant-based diet for short-term weight loss because giving up animal products and junk food often results in significant shedding of pounds. While I was never extremely overweight, I found that within the first three months of switching to a vegan diet I had lost 15 pounds, effortlessly. I was eating a TON of food, but it was all high-fiber and low calorie, so I was filling up without fattening up. My primary care physician at the time, Dr. H. Robert Silverstein, supported my transition and instilled in me the mantra, "Gorge till you're gorgeous!"

Many of my personal chef clients who come to me with the goal of losing weight often find that within three weeks they immediately see results. Then they think they're done and can return to "normal." Unfortunately, this method often leads to a health setback and return to bad eating habits. This is why I stress that eating vegan should be considered more of a lifestyle change instead of a diet and to always think of the implications of your food choices that extend beyond your plate.

By becoming vegan you are refusing to participate in a system that exploits and causes suffering to animals as well as to the workers who are desensitized to daily brutality on the slaughterhouse floor, minimizing your impact on limited environmental resources such as land and water, reducing environmental pollution caused by factory farms and processing facilities, and improving your own physical, mental, and spiritual health. Eating vegan is far superior to cage-free; it's karma-free. It's simply a matter of asking yourself the question, "Do I love animals?" If the answer is an unequivocal "YES!" then ask yourself, "Should any animal unnecessarily suffer because of me?" Could you be a witness to that suffering and do nothing? Ten billion animals are tortured and killed every year in the U.S. alone, and while we can't save them all, we can reject a system that allows this type of violence and exploitation to occur on a daily basis. They need you to be a hero.

> I became a vegetarian after realizing that animals feel afraid, cold, hungry and unhappy like we do. I feel very deeply about vegetarianism and the animal kingdom. It was my dog Boycott who led me to question the right of humans to eat other sentient beings.
>
> ~ César Chávez

Chapter 2

"I don't know where to begin!!"

HELP!! I Need Somebody

One of the most common complaints I hear about switching to a vegan diet is not knowing where to begin. The decision alone often feels so overwhelming, but if you've already set your mind to it, BRAVO! You've taken the first step. The rest is easy. That is, once you get over the fear of creating magic in your kitchen.

Whatever way you begin your vegan journey, it's always the best way for you. The point is that you are your own guide. Whether it's for health reasons that you're making the transition, or you're taking it gradually one day a week and cutting back on meat, or you're shooting for full lifestyle immersion into veganism for ethical reasons, know that you have chosen a path that will reduce the amount of suffering in the world.

To make it easy on yourself, follow the advice of the wise Buddhist nun, Pema Chodron, and "start where you are." Some of you come to vegan cooking as seasoned chefs already possessing knife skills and a familiarity with kitchen equipment, so you may want simply to peruse these steps for items relevant to your needs as a vegan. Others are equally new to vegan cooking as you are to cooking in general, and you may want to consider this as a detailed step-by-step guide. Most of you are probably somewhere in between, having dabbled in vegan cooking for awhile and come here looking for fresh ideas. Whatever the case may be, grounding yourself where you are and using these tips as guidance will help you build a strong foundation upon which future cooking endeavors will be laid.

Kitchen Essentials

You don't need the most expensive, top of the line products to make good food, but in the case of kitchen equipment, you often get what you pay for. That said, I will make recommendations for various budgets as well as offer my personal preferences as suggestions. These are the tools I've come to favor over the years, but that doesn't necessarily mean that others aren't equally good. It also doesn't mean you need to splurge on everything all at once! Buy what you're comfortable with when starting out, upgrade when necessary, and consider every purchase an investment. You will be much happier using equipment you don't have to fight with.

It's important to equip your kitchen with the right tools of the trade so that you'll not only be safe and feel comfortable, but also so that you'll come to enjoy the cooking process itself and not see it as yet another chore to muddle through. When I first started out in my own kitchen prior to becoming a personal chef, I didn't even have a cutting board. I used to hold an apple in the palm of my left hand and pray that the serrated steak knife I was gingerly holding in my right hand wouldn't slip. Yes, it was bad. But if I can get over the hurdle, so can you.

Appliances Take care of the major investments by equipping your kitchen with the right appliances based on your budget. I survived with a hand-me-down blender and $29.99 Black & Decker food processor for years before I became fully committed to vegan cooking.

- **Food processor** - Get the biggest you can afford (I recommend 14-cup) as this will save time when making large batches of mixtures such as pate, nut crusts, nut cheeses, and bean dips. Cuisinart is a reliable standard.
- **High speed blender** - I use mine nearly every day for smoothies, sauces, and nut milks. You can get by with something basic like a Waring, and even the Ninja is a highly rated blender, but when you're feeling confident and ready to splurge, go with the Vita-Mix. You can save a little money by buying it reconditioned directly from the manufacturer's website.
- **Immersion blender** - For pureeing hot soups to a smooth consistency, this is indispensable. If you get one with a bowl attachment, you can also use it for processing smaller jobs. This is great for making a whipped "cream" or single serving of sauce. I take it with me wherever I cook because it's much easier to transport than my blender and food processor. An immersion blender with attachments is also a decent, affordable option before you're ready to purchase two separate appliances. Cuisinart and Braun are some good manufacturers.

Tools These essential tools will make cooking easy and fun, and you'll feel like a pro when you use them.
- knives - 8" chef's knife, serrated knife, paring knife
- knife sharpener and honing steel
- skillet - 10" stainless steel, 10" non-stick, 10" cast iron
- pots - Dutch oven (6 qt), 5-6 qt. pasta pot, 1-2 qt. sauce pot with lids
- metal colander
- mixing bowls, measuring cups (wet and dry) and measuring spoons
- wooden cutting board

Gadgets I'm not a fan of gadgets that serve just one purpose, but these essentials will make kitchen chores a breeze. Except where noted, I really like OXO brand for most of these.

- garlic press (Zyliss is the best)
- metal tongs
- metal and plastic spatulas
- wooden spoons of different sizes
- ladle
- vegetable peeler & zester
- grater
- mandolin slicer (a basic one is about $20)
- saladacco spiral slicer "spiralizer" (Joyce Chen has one for about $20-30)

Pantry Staples Stock your pantry with staples that are versatile, healthful, and have a long shelf life so you'll be ready for any kitchen emergency.

- bulk grains (brown rice, quinoa, millet, wild rice, amaranth, teff, corn meal)
- bulk nuts & seeds (almonds, walnuts, pecans, pistachios, pine nuts, pumpkin seeds, sunflower seeds, sesame seeds, flax seeds, chia seeds, hemp seeds)
- bulk dry legumes (black-eyed peas, brown lentil, French lentil, red lentil)
- pasta (Italian style, rice noodles, soba noodles)
- canned tomatoes (Muir Glen fire-roasted are fabulous) and beans (black, butter, kidney, cannelini, pinto, garbanzo)
- non-dairy milks (rice, almond, hemp, coconut, soy)
- sea vegetables (nori sheets, dulse flakes, arame)
- oils (olive, toasted sesame, canola, coconut)
- condiments (balsamic vinegar, apple cider vinegar, Dijon mustard, yellow mustard, Sriracha hot sauce, tamari, pickles, nut butters, tahini, jam, etc.)

- bulk herbs and spices (basil, oregano, rosemary, cumin, chili powder, coriander, turmeric, curry powder, garlic powder, onion powder, nutritional yeast)
- flour, corn starch, baking soda, baking powder
- sweeteners (agave syrup, rice syrup, maple syrup, evaporated cane juice)

Personally, I recommend holding off on stocking your pantry with dessert ingredients such as flours, sweeteners, and chocolate, partly because they're expensive, but mostly because I believe desserts should be kept to a minimum. While they're yummy and sexy and everyone loves a decadent vegan cupcake, a goal of a good vegan chef should be to stay healthy and balanced.

This is where I began 17 years ago. You will learn what your favorites are the more you practice. Oh, and one more thing. While this isn't really a necessity, sometimes a little indulgence will make cooking all that much more fun. For me, that means a cute little apron. Or maybe some fluffy, super-absorbent hand towels. Or an Emile Henry casserole dish. Whatever brings out your joy will show in the finished product. Be inspired.

Keeping a Tidy Kitchen

Have you ever walked into your kitchen at the end of the evening and thought that a tornado must have hit while you were eating dinner? Or worse, you haven't even begun cooking and you're already on the phone to FEMA? I've been there, many times. The answer to your dilemma may not be emergency relief, but instead, a few simple steps that you can take to prevent a disaster from happening in the future.

One of the unspoken taboos that stresses most chefs is a messy kitchen. Not only is it impossible to get any work done in a kitchen filled with chaos, but it's also de-energizing, demoralizing, and downright depressing. Sadly, the energy that surrounds you is also what ends up going into your food, and nobody wants a plate full of that.

Remember, your kitchen is a sanctuary. It's where you not only prepare food for yourself and your family, but it's also a place for peace and tranquility. Strive to create a space filled with order and harmony so that your kitchen can nurture you just as the food does, leaving you nourished and satisfied. But don't be hard on yourself if you can't measure up to Martha Stewart! While I'm not always perfect in this arena, I know that the discipline of making the effort results in a sense of empowerment that translates to all aspects of my life, and that's a good thing.

Before

- **Get organized.** Have a designated space for everything you use on a regular basis (food processor, cutting board, measuring cups, etc.), and return everything to its place when done.

- **Clean, well-lighted space.** Make sure you have adequate lighting both overhead and above work areas so that you can see your veggies as you're cutting them and know whether they're cooking properly in the pan. You don't want to go from translucent to burned because you can't see your onions!

- **Be open.** Keep open shelves or overhead racks for your pots, pans, lid covers, located near your stove so you can find them when you need them. Stock pantry staples on open, lined shelves in clear, labeled containers for easy access.

- **Hold it.** Store cooking utensils in a canister by the stove or in a storage bin and measuring cups and spoons in drawers or on shelves near your work area for easy access.

- **De-clutter.** Remove that pile of mail, all those cooking magazines, and the kids' homework from your countertops. Always keep your cutting board clean and the area next to your stove clear. Your kitchen is for cooking; it's not life's storage bin!

- **Keep in line.** Store frequently used electric appliances in a neat row along the back of the countertop against the wall so they can be pulled forward when needed, then pushed back into place when done.

During

- **Clean as you go.** Use your time in the kitchen wisely by cleaning up while something on the stove is cooking. Whether it's washing pots in the sink, wiping the countertop, or picking up stray veggies that didn't make it into the pan, your eye should be focused on tidying up those little messes so they don't become catastrophes.

- **Spooning.** Keep stirring spoon, tongs, spatulas and other utensils close at hand by the stovetop, and always have one designated tasting spoon at the ready.

- **Wear it well.** Keep yourself neat and tidy by always wearing an apron, and drape a hand-towel at your waist or over a shoulder for quick cleanup of those sudden messes.

After

- **Go home.** Return everything to its proper place (pantry items, equipment, utensils, etc.) as soon as you're done using it.

- **Neat-o.** Wipe countertops, cutting boards, stovetop, and oven once the meal is completed. Don't wait until messes become dried on layers of cement that need to be chiseled away late at night.

- **Clean as a whistle.** Toss apron, towels and other linens in the laundry after each use. Do a quick sweep and mop of the floor. Return your cookbooks to the bookshelf (or at least on your nightstand).

- **Take a break.** You deserve it. After creating a meal for yourself or your family, it's always nice to sit back at the end of the evening and commend yourself for a job well done.

"

Often when you think you're
at the end of something, you're
at the beginning of something else.

~ Fred Rogers

"

Chapter 3

"It's so expensive! I can't afford it!!"

You Work Hard for the Money

A major concern people have when switching to a vegan diet is that it will be expensive. Yes, maybe so, but there are two ways of looking at this. One, you're buying real food that is high quality, so you're getting what you paid for. And two, you're worth it. Don't ever skimp when it comes to your health. When you buy organic plant-based ingredients, you're not only taking care of your own body, but you're also taking care of the entire ecosystem in which the food grew: the soil that is enriched, the bees and butterflies that helped pollinate the plants, and the farmers who grew it without exposing themselves to toxic chemicals. While that may cost more, what you pay for is more than just a quick meal; it is voting for what you believe in with your hard-earned dollar. That said, there are ways to stretch your limited cash without feeling deprived or needing to clip coupons (most of which are for chemical-laden junk you don't need anyway).

12 Ways to Be a Thrifty Vegan

I learned to shop on a budget when I became vegan because I had a modest income at the time. Cost was my greatest obstacle when I first made the switch, but I developed a system of saving money without feeling deprived. I use this same philosophy when

I do the shopping for my business. I always want to get the best price while stretching limited resources, yet never sacrifice quality. Here are some of my secret methods for getting the most for your money.

1. **Buy in bulk.** Grains, dried beans, nuts, seeds, dried herbs and spices are always cheapest when you purchase from the bulk bins at health food stores. Take as much or as little as you need. If your recipe calls for 1 tablespoon of cumin, just put that amount in a little baggie instead of buying an entire jar which may get stale before you use it up. If there's a sale, stock up. All of these items can be stored in your own jars on pantry shelves or in the fridge.

2. **Shop locally and in season.** When there's an abundance of seasonal produce, it's usually at its cheapest. Buy as much as you can afford, then freeze or dehydrate whatever you can't eat to enjoy later in the year.

3. **Pick Your Own.** I always take advantage of PYO produce such as blueberries, strawberries, and raspberries when in season because they're ridiculously expensive otherwise. I spend a sunny summer afternoon picking bags of berries, then freeze a bunch to enjoy in the dearth of winter.

4. **Chill Out.** Frozen fruits and veggies are often cheaper to buy when not in season. Stock your freezer with fruits like berries, mango, and papaya for making smoothies, and bags of frozen spinach and other veggies which are perfect time-saving alternatives for making soups.

5. **Make friends with a farmer/gardener.** While farmers' markets aren't always the cheapest way to shop for groceries, sometimes you can get bargains on those seconds that get picked over by everyone else. I've actually scored a huge box of produce -- for FREE -- during the last few minutes when the farmer was packing up his truck.

6. **Hunt for "secret sales."** Many people spend Sunday afternoons scouring store circulars for coupons and specials. That's a start, but what I really mean is look for those "secret sales." My independent grocery store offers a 10% discount on cases of canned goods and cereal, and because I shop there on nearly a daily basis, I get 10% off of everything. The key is that it never hurts to ask. In addition, discount retailers such as Ocean State Job Lot often carry pantry staples such as Bob's Red Mill gluten-free flour at reduced prices.

7. **Join a co-op or buying club.** Sometimes mail order pricing is closer to wholesale than retail. If you can find a few friends to shop online with, you can split the shipping costs and save big bucks. A good place to look is United Natural Foods on-line (http://www.unitedbuyingclubs.com).

8. **Mail order.** If you need a bunch of pantry staples like peanut butter, olive oil, condiments, and even those few splurges like Sweet & Sara marshmallows, online retailers like Vegan Essentials are sometimes cheaper than grocery stores. Plus they often have sales on discontinued items or new products.

9. **Cook in quantity.** I often designate Sunday as my batch cooking day for making huge pots of soups, stews, and grains that can be eaten later in the week or even frozen. It's not only economical, but it saves time and energy as well.

11. **Grow your own.** Even if you don't have a big sunny yard for a garden, a community garden is one of the cheapest ways to grow produce for yourself and your family by maximizing yield and minimizing labor and expense. If you only have room for a few pots of plants out on a windowsill, growing your own greens, herbs, edible flowers, and sprouts can save money on some typically expensive ingredients. And whatever you don't use right away can either be dried or frozen for later.

12. **Save seeds and cuttings.** The veggies we get from the grocery store are still alive and some will continue to grow. When you've cut off the leaves of your head of Romaine, you can pop the stem end in a shallow dish of water and it will sprout new leaves. (Just remember to change the water every day.) Onions and celery will grow shoots that can be cut and used in your soups and sautes, and tops of beets and turnips will sprout greens that are highly nutritious.

Quality Ingredients In, Quality Product Out

Remember that in the quest for reducing expenses, you must never sacrifice quality. This should be a mantra. You know those great big containers of 99¢ spices you see on the shelf at your local discount store? Don't buy them! They are most likely irradiated to enhance shelf-life and they will have very little flavor. And if you're hoping to get some medicinal benefits, forget about it. Although oil of oregano is a potent antibiotic and anti-fungal in its fresh, organic form, dried leaves that have been denatured will have none of those qualities. In fact, they may even contain trace residues of pesticides.

Also avoid soup starters, bouillon, spice mixes, vegetable broth, and other processed food bases, even if they're organic. Many of these are extremely high in sodium, and some may even contain Monosodium Glutamate (MSG), a concentrated flavor enhancer that can cause numerous adverse reactions in the body[1]. It is often hidden in ingredient labels under names such as "yeast extract," "hydrolyzed vegetable protein," "glutamic acid," "modified food starch," and "soy extracts." Plus, they're expensive. Instead of paying $5 for a quart of vegetable broth, you can make your own stock with the Holy Trinity of carrots, onion, and celery simmered in water till soft - for pennies per serving[2]. Never buy jarred pasta sauce or salsa again once you learn how simple it is to make from scratch. And it's much cheaper, fresher, and healthier for you.

---

1. "One of the best overviews of the very real dangers of MSG comes from Dr. Russell Blaylock, a board-certified neurosurgeon and author of Excitotoxins: The Taste that Kills. In it he explains that MSG is an excitotoxin, which means it overexcites your cells to the point of damage or death, causing brain damage to varying degrees -- and potentially even triggering or worsening learning disabilities, Alzheimer's disease, Parkinson's disease, Lou Gehrig's disease and more." Dr. Joseph Mercola, "MSG: Is This Silent Killer Lurking in Your Kitchen Cabinets?" Huffington Post, January 29, 2014.

2. "The FDA requires that foods containing added MSG list it in the ingredient panel on the packaging as monosodium glutamate. However, MSG occurs naturally in ingredients such as hydrolyzed vegetable protein, autolyzed yeast, hydrolyzed yeast, yeast extract, soy extracts, and protein isolate, as well as in tomatoes and cheeses. While FDA requires that these products be listed on the ingredient panel, the agency does not require the label to also specify that they naturally contain MSG." [www.FDA.gov]

> Earth is not a platform
> for human life. It's a living being.
> We're not on it but a part of it.
> Its health is our health.
>
> ~ Thomas Moore

Chapter 4

"I just don't have the time."

Time Is on Your Side

When first switching to a vegan diet, the learning curve can feel like a jack-knifed trailer in the road. Yes, it can be challenging to absorb so much new information, ingredients, substitutions, and techniques. Any new endeavor can feel overwhelming at first. Always remember, however, your goal is not to become a celebrity vegan chef. You just want to learn a few simple recipes to get you through the week (in the beginning, anyway). The time it takes you to cook a Standard American Diet (SAD) meal is the same amount of time it will take you to cook a happy vegan meal. The recipes in this cookbook are purposefully quick and easy so that you won't feel the pressure of another cumbersome chore added to your busy schedule.

Zen Mind

I can't emphasize enough how important it is to minimize and manage stress in our lives. Whether it's through meditation, yoga, positive visualization, kickboxing, running, or any other technique you've developed to help keep a calm and peaceful mind, this is the state you want to achieve when approaching your cooking. Now, I understand that's difficult after a long day at work or with several screaming kids running around underfoot, but it's nevertheless essential to preparing a meal that everyone will love. Although it sounds counterintuitive, it's surprising how much time suddenly becomes available once you slow down.

Consider it the Zen of vegan cooking.

Imagine where your food came from, how the plants grew in the soil, and were nurtured by the sun and the rain. Feel the energy that Mother Nature put into growing each luscious vegetable. Touch them and take a moment to hold them in your hand, paying attention to the texture, shape, and weight. Expand your senses by examining them visually and envisioning a rainbow on your plate, then notice their aromas. The bright, sour note of citrus peel always perks me up. And fresh herbs like basil and oregano always transport me to my grandma's Italian kitchen. As you move through each step of the cooking process, come back to these thoughts to help ground you and connect back to who you are: a vegan chef.

6 Time-saving Tips to Save Your Sanity in the Kitchen

The life of a restaurant chef is frantic, hectic, stressful, and chaotic. This is seen as "normal" in the industry, and in many cases even desirable. It is anything but healthy. While the fast-paced world of a busy commercial kitchen may demand this, it does not mean you need to bring these qualities to your own kitchen. You are not churning out meal after meal of the same 15-20 appetizers and entrees for 10 hours straight, keeping up with orders as they fly in and fly out, prepping, saucing, sauteing and plating. You do not have a whole crew working for you, managing every move they make. If you've panicked at the thought of doing this in your own kitchen, pushing yourself to exhaustion while slave-driving family members to cut up veggies, remember, you're not on TV. You are cooking for your family, your loved ones, people who know you and know who you are. Share positive vegan qualities of a peaceful mind, compassion, joy, and love with them and it will come through in your food. Namaste.

Below are some time-saving tips I use on a daily basis when preparing a week's worth of meals in the client's kitchen.

1. **Get organized** (mentally and physically) before cooking. Read through your recipe(s) and ingredient lists thoroughly to determine the sequence of steps, total time allowance, and how to orchestrate the multi-tasking of components. Identify which ingredients are from your pantry and which are from the refrigerator, and place all of them on the countertop. Breathe! Do a few yoga stretches!

2. **Mis en place.** Arrange ingredients on your countertop in categorized regions according to usage. Your most frequently used staples such as olive oil, sea salt, and black pepper should be placed next to the stove for ease of use. Produce that needs to be washed and peeled should be next to the sink, then left in a colander to dry.

3. **Location, Location, Location.** To minimize walking, the ultimate wasteful time-sapper, your cutting board should ideally be located on the countertop between the stove and the sink. If this is not possible, then placing it next to the stove is best. A table or island situated between the sink and stove can provide additional counter space as well as reduce footsteps. Your goal is to be able to pivot on a dime.

4. **Multi-task the cooking process.** Work backwards by reading through your recipe(s) first, then start with the most time-consuming component. Prep all of your veggies first, then cook them later. Work on several recipes at once (you have 4-6 burners - use them all!). Preheat and get baking, and set your timer if you need an audible reminder.

5. **Clean as you go.** There's nothing worse than a messy stovetop and dirty dishes in the sink after a long day of work followed by a night of cooking. Minimize this stress by cleaning as you go. Place leftovers in containers and allow them to cool on the countertop before sealing and placing them in the fridge.

6. **Put everything back where it belongs.** Reseal and return pantry items to their shelves. Slide electronics to the back of the countertop. Store unused produce in containers and bags and put them in your fridge or freezer immediately.

> A man can live and be
> healthy without killing animals
> for food; therefore, if he eats meat,
> he participates in taking
> animal life merely for the
> sake of his appetite.
>
> ~ Leo Tolstoy

Chapter 5

"Isn't vegan food boring?"

Color Me Impressed

We've all heard the expression "you eat with your eyes," and this is particularly true when it comes to vegan food. There is a common misconception that vegan food is bland, boring, and beige. I think this sentiment lingers from the hippie days when brown rice, tofu and granola were the staples, and frankly, if I ate that way I'd be pretty bored, too. But we've come a long way, baby!! Fortunately today our produce options have greatly expanded; we can get seasonal, local fruits and veggies just as easily as exotic delicacies imported from the Tropics, and they're all delicious and gorgeous. Cooking vegan food becomes an adventure with a veritable rainbow on our plates.

Creating Culinary Balance: Color, Taste and Texture

I'm sure we've all had the experience of being served a plate of beige food, whether it's rice and beans or meat and potatoes. There's nothing there to make us say "WOW!!" Not only is there a monotone of color, but the texture is also limp and listless. It's hard to get excited when the food in front of you just looks like a pile of mush and tastes like it, too.

To get excited about food, it's important to have balance of color, taste, and texture. This makes us feel satisfied, and it also eliminates cravings. Think about the typical SAD snack of super salty chips or pretzels. If you eat this way all of the time, you will crave the polar opposite of sweets in an attempt to find equilibrium. This often means you will wash down that salty junk food with a can of soda. Conversely, if you crave bread and baked goods all the time, the more you eat, the less satisfied you will feel because the underlying craving will still remain. Any time the food you eat is isolated in the extremes, it creates imbalance in your body. To achieve balance, you must incorporate a variety of foods into your diet which will satisfy you nutritionally as well.

- **Color** When creating a meal, think about how it will look on your plate. Envision the Color Wheel and complementary colors that work well when paired together. You want vibrant, contrasting colors such as red and green, like tomatoes tossed with kale in a Mediterranean Quinoa Pilaf, or the bright pop of Roasted Red Pepper Coulis to dress up Baked Stuffed Zucchini. Warm hued vegetables like carrot, butternut squash, or yellow squash intensify a plate and stimulate the appetite. Fresh chopped scallion or cilantro scattered for garnish create visual interest in an otherwise ordinary dish.

- **Taste** Ultimately, the food has to taste good. And although the culinary tradition of loading it with salt and butter may enhance the flavor inherent in a dish, this approach negates the subtlety of our palate - and it's also quite unhealthy. Every meal you create should strive for flavor balance of the four tastes: salty, sweet, sour, and bitter, plus the occasional kick of spice and umami for that savory quality. A simple salad often combines these flavors: sour lemon, sweet agave syrup, olive oil for umami, and a pinch of salt on top of bitter greens. Think about the flavor profile you are creating every time you put together a meal. If it seems like "something's missing," consult your taste palate.

- **Texture** Sometimes all I feel like eating is something crunchy. It doesn't mater if it's a carrot or a cookie; I just want to bite into something that has snap. This is fine for a snack; however, when planning a meal, it helps to have a variety of textures to add a little intrigue. Including an array of crispy, crunchy, chewy, hard, soft, smooth, creamy, and silky textures in your meals gives your mouth a workout and stimulates your brain. A variety of textures makes food more interesting and ultimately more satisfying. Try garnishing a silky vegetable bisque soup with toasted pumpkin seeds, pair a smooth dipping sauce with crunchy vegetable crudites, or make a base of creamy polenta for crispy cornmeal crusted tofu. My Cruciferous Vegetable Slaw is a good example of a salad that combines several different textures by including crispy broccoli, cauliflower and cabbage, hard and crunchy pumpkin seeds, chewy dried cranberries, soft and smooth avocado, and a silky cashew cream dressing. People have commented that this tastes like a one-dish meal it's so satisfying.

Recipe Versatility

Food becomes exciting when it is prepared in a multitude of ways. Rather than having the same old rice and beans 4 nights in a row, why not try transforming it into a creative presentation? You can use the same rice and beans as a stuffing for baked zucchini boats, or layer it with veggies and cover with a cashew cheese sauce to turn it into a casserole, or add a tomato-based broth and veggies to create a soup, or even add different spices to transform a Mexican staple into an Indian curry. These are just some simple ways the same base can be modified to create several different meals, all unique unto themselves.

I often cook up a big pot of veggies in a soup base of carrot, onion, and celery on a Sunday, then I change it up through the week. On Monday I take a serving out and season it with basil and oregano like a minestrone. The next day I use Mexican spices like cumin and chili powder, add some black beans, and serve it with quinoa. The third day I mix a serving with curry powder, turmeric, coconut milk, and a squeeze of lemon to make an Indian curry over brown rice. On day four I might combine the veggies with a creamy white sauce and toss them with pasta. For each of these, a garnish of fresh herbs adds brightness and color to liven up the meal. Nothing boring and ordinary about that.

Our doubts are traitors,
and make us lose the good
we oft might win, by fearing to attempt.

- William Shakespeare

Chapter 6

"What will my friends think?"

Get the Party Started

We vegans are known for our partying! Well... I don't know about that. But it's pretty nice to be able to create delicious food and share it with people you care about. I often host seasonal potlucks -- New Year's Day Brunch, Vernal Equinox Cleanse, Summer Solstice Picnic -- where the menu is based on what's appropriate for that occasion. My New Year's Brunch is famous for its pancakes. In the summer, we picnic on raw foods fresh from the garden. Whatever the reason, make a point to get together with others to create a community of compassion and spread the joy of vegan cooking. You'll be surprised at how fun it can be when you include friends in your new endeavor.

Choreographing a Multi-Course Menu

Once you've honed your cooking skills and have a few tried and true recipes under your belt, you may be giddy enough to want to show off your creations to friends and family. This is the true test of being vegan under pressure: keeping cool in the kitchen while surrounded by chaos.

There are times when you may need to cook several recipes at once, whether it's a fancy four-course dinner for that special someone, an evening meal for your family after a long day at work, or a dinner party with friends. You'll want to manage your time effectively and efficiently to get food on the table with nary a hair out of place or bead of sweat on your brow. If the thought of creating a multi-course menu fills you with the same amount of dread as it does excitement and makes you abandon the idea of even attempting such a crazy notion, fear not. These tips will keep you from falling into the weeds.

Try to do all of the creative fun stuff like decorating and printing menus a few days before The Big Day so you don't have to worry about it when preparing the food for your guests. This minimizes the stress of trying to do everything all at once. It will also help you get in the mood while you're shopping when you imagine how everything will be arranged on the tables and envision your guests joyfully sipping cocktails and raving about the amazing food you've prepared for them. This works for me all the time.

1. **Plan ahead.** Try to do all of the grocery shopping a day or two ahead so you can devote full attention to prepping for and cooking the meal on the day of the party. Review your final menu to determine if anything can be done the day before, such as soaking nuts or baking a dessert.

2. **Make a list.** Sometimes it helps to write out your game plan as a check list. Identify which step(s) in each recipe that need to be done in advance, such as preheating an oven or marinating tofu, and start with those first, then work backwards. Determine which step will take the longest, such as cooking brown rice, and do that next. Each item you check off will feel like a mini-accomplishment worthy of celebration.

3. **Prep first, cook later.** When cooking several recipes at once, it helps to do the prepping for all of them first, such as washing all of your veggies at once, bringing a pot of water to a boil in order to blanch them, and peeling and cutting the veggies and placing them in separate containers until ready for use.

4. **Multi-task the cooking process.** Take advantage of all of the burners on your stove and pre-cook several recipes at once. Start the precooking in a large sauté pan on the front burner closest to your cutting board. Move the sauté pan to a side burner to do the finish cooking while starting the precooking of a 2nd recipe on the front burner. As recipes are completed, move them to a back burner, hot plate, or countertop to keep warm while completing the remaining recipes.

5. **Make every moment count by making use of every moment**. While waiting for a pot of water to boil, wash, peel and cut veggies. While onions are sautéing in a skillet, prep the sauce. If you have a full stovetop and something cooking in the oven, move to your cleaning station and tidy up.

Dress It Up

The ordinary can become special with a few simple additions. I like to call it "Component Cooking." Start with a humble dish like Three Sisters Stew on Polenta and dress it up with a colorful sauce like Parsley Pistou, then top with a sprinkle of Toasted Spiced Pepitas. For dessert, take a basic brownie and drizzle the plate with Raspberry Coulis and Chocolate Sauce, then top with a big scoop of coconut milk ice cream and garnish with toasted coconut flakes and fresh berries. The components are elevated to create a gourmet presentation, with very little effort. This is how you transform everyday recipes into vegan feasts. I often start with a concept or theme that's based on the season or holiday. Here are some ideas to get you started partying like a vegan.

- **Valentine's Day** Some thoughts that immediately come to mind for this holiday are red foods, chocolate, and aphrodisiacs such as avocado, asparagus, spices, and dates. The meal I would create would be built around simple recipes dressed up for the occasion. Menu: Romaine Lettuce Leaf and Avocado Salad with Mock Caesar Dressing; Tofu Piccata, Mashed Potatoes and Roasted Asparagus with a drizzle of Parsley Pistou; Chocolate Chocolate Chip Brownie with Raspberry Coulis, Chocolate Sauce, fresh Berries, and a sprinkle of cinnamon and cocoa powder to decorate the plate.

- **St. Patrick's Day** Green is the theme for this holiday. Start with a Massaged Kale Salad with Granny Smith Apple, Avocado and Hemp Seeds. For the entree, serve Crispy Cornmeal Crusted Tofu with Mushroom Gravy and a side of Colcannon.

- **Vernal Equinox** This is the time of year to be thinking about a cleanse. Focus on light, raw foods that are in season. Menu: Asparagus Bisque Soup garnished with Pea Shoots; Chickpea Croquettes with Tahini Lemon Sauce; Quinoa Pilaf with Spring Vegetables.

- **Summer Picnic in the Raw** This is my favorite time of year, and I let the garden dictate the menu. When summer vegetables like zucchini are in abundance, it's time to get out the spiralizer. Menu: Nasturtium Leaf Cannoli with Macadamia "Rawcotta;" Zucchini Ribbons with Cashew Cheese Béchamel and Sun-dried Tomato Marinara; Strawberry Shortcake with Tapioca Cream.

- **Holiday Time** If you're planning a party for the holidays, think of finger food as well as entrees that can be made in large portions and served out of trays. This will minimize the work involved with preparing food for the masses. Also consider components of your meal that can be utilized in a variety of ways. For example, Olive Tapenade can be spread on crostini, stirred into a dip with pureed cannelini beans for crudites, used as a filling with roasted veggies in wraps, and tossed with pasta, beans, cherry tomatoes, and baby spinach for a simple main dish.

- **New Year's Brunch** I like to start the new year by indulging in warming comfort food. To me, this is the perfect way to cozy up with friends and family and relax after a night of partying. Menu: Perfect Pumpkin Pancakes with Maple Pecan Praline; Southwestern Tofu Scramble; Mango Salsa; Home-fried Smoked Paprika Potatoes with Sriracha; Blueberry Streusel Muffins.

"For beautiful eyes, look for the
good in others; for beautiful lips,
speak only words of kindness;
and for poise, walk with the knowledge
that you are never alone.

~ Audrey Hepburn

Chapter 7

"It's too hard!!!"

Ain't No Mountain High Enough

There will be times on your vegan journey when you'll feel as if you've reached a roadblock and can't go any further. Maybe you've gotten into a rut of cooking the same old tired recipes over and over. Perhaps you're living in a household filled with picky eaters and every meal becomes a fight. Or you just couldn't resist the temptation of that slice of Pepe's pizza. Whatever the hurdle, know that you're not alone.

Sometimes the journey feels like a steep, mountainous climb that will challenge your resolve at every corner. Becoming vegan is often a battle against the tide of a society which endeavors to get you to take the easy way out by conforming to bad habits and perpetuating suffering in the world. Stay strong. Focus on the good habits you are establishing and positive karma that results.

A friend and colleague of mine, Dr. Joel Marks, recently celebrated his five-year "veganversary" on New Year's Day. He is still going strong and has taken his personal choice to a new level by advocating for animals and sharing his epiphanies in a blog called The Easy Vegan (www.TheEasyVegan.com). He writes about his conscious decision to align his actions with his beliefs, his successful transition to veganism, and the many unexpected benefits (the food really does taste good).

"I myself decided to take the plunge a year ago. It was my new year's resolution. I did not exactly go cold turkey, so to speak, because I had abstained from eating mammals for decades. But my original motivation had been health and humanitarian. I had read about the cholesterol advantages of avoiding meat, and also about the inefficient production of protein by feeding grains to animals in a world where millions of people were starving.

Only much more recently did I learn about factory farming, and also that by far the most numerous abused creatures on this planet are poultry and fish. There was nothing for it, then, but to give up eating all animals as well as dairy and eggs."

~ Dr. Joel Marks

If you're determined to fulfill a vegan resolution – for your own health, for the sake of the animals, or because you care about the future of our planet – let me offer a few tips for staying on track. Remember, be practical. Every journey begins with that first step.

7 Habits of Highly Effective Vegans

1. **Set specific goals.** Decide if you want to go "cold turkey" or take it slow and steady. Maybe you might want to give "Meatless Mondays" a try. Then gradually add one more day each week. Or maybe you could start with that favorite food that you think is impossible to give up, like cheese, for example - always a tough one (thank heavens for cashew cheese!). Do what works best for you.

2. **Be mindful of what you eat.** The simple act of thinking about food and where it comes from has a tremendous impact on what goes into your mouth. When you find yourself saying, "Do I really want to eat that?" you will have come a long way. Check in with yourself to see how you're doing and how you're feeling. Those who keep food diaries have the most success when changing their eating habits.

3. **Do some research.** Vegan cookbooks, blogs, and websites are plentiful. You could spend a lifetime reading them. Fortunately, most of the work has been done for you. It's simply a matter of browsing for what appeals to you. Try one new recipe a week. Go to vegan potluck dinners. Share your favorites with friends and family. They'll love you for it (especially if you bring desserts).

4. **Discover new restaurants.** Make dining out a pleasure by experimenting with ethnic cuisine (Thai, Ethiopian, Japanese, Mexican, and Indian have many delicious options) or go to your favorite places and ask the chef if he/she can create a vegan dish for you. Most major cities have numerous dining options for vegans. For a listing of veg-friendly establishments, visit Happy Cow (www.happycow.net), VegGuide (www.VegGuide.org), or Veg Dining (www.vegdining.com). Explore!

5. **Find a buddy.** It always helps to know someone who is making the vegan transition at the same time so you can help each other out. Talk to someone who has been there before (I've been through it all, just ask). Connect on Facebook and Twitter with other vegans and build an international community. Or look online on Meetup.com to find vegan groups in your own neighborhood and

make some new friends.

6. **Enjoy your food.** Really. It's new. It's different. And you don't have to feel deprived. You will soon discover an amazing array of options you never dreamed existed. Who could possibly be upset about eating Eggplant Rollatini with Macadamia Ricotta, Fire-Roasted Tomato Marinara and drizzled with Parsley Oil?

7. **Be kind to yourself.** Your choice to adopt a vegan diet is a big decision and will require dedication. Don't worry if you "fall off the wagon" or "cheat." It's not a guilt trip. It's not about perfection. Every little thing you can do to minimize the suffering of animals, improve your health, and respect the environment has a positive impact on all those around you. The effect multiplies. And you'll feel pretty good in the process.

Preventing Vegan Burnout

At some point it's inevitable that you consider the impact of your choices and become overwhelmed by the idea of no longer being complicit in routine acts of violence inflicted upon animals in the agriculture industry. Sometimes this feeling can be exhilarating: it's empowering to free yourself of systematic suffering and exploitation. At other times, it can be discouraging, with the gnawing sense that no matter how much you do for animals, you can't save them all. As a vegan activist, it's often difficult to balance hope with reality, to be able to persevere and stay positive despite all odds stacked against you. And there are times when the sadness of the world drags you so far down that you feel like you're trying to bail out a sinking ship with a Dixie cup. Believe me, I've been there. And I've somehow managed to pull myself out and get back in the game, fighting the good fight, for the animals. Whenever you get that discouraged feeling inside, remember to follow these tips.

- **Take care of yourself.** Only you can do that. Stay strong by giving yourself lots of love and encouragement. Any moment you're feeling down, remind yourself you're pretty awesome. An "I love you" thought bubble once in awhile doesn't hurt either. Even if you can't see it immediately, everything you're doing does make a difference, within your circles and beyond. Focus on your successes, and be assured that there will be many more.

- **Take a break.** Disconnect from media and electronic devices. While it's important to be informed, sometimes social media and television can become distractions. Or worse, they suck your spirit dry. Set time limits and stay in balance to prevent that deadly addiction from taking over your life.

- **Take a hike.** Reconnect with Mother Nature. Remember, the reason why we're here on this planet is that we're all a part of the greater ecosystem. If you've been neglecting that crucial connection, step outdoors, smell the fresh air, feel the sun on your face, and remember to breathe.

> I always wondered why somebody
> doesn't do something about that.
> Then I realized I was somebody.
>
> ~ Lily Tomlin

~ The Recipes ~

Prelude: Salads, Soups, & Starters

Verse: On the Side

Chorus: Main Dishes

Bridge: Sauces, Gravies & Glazes

Coda: Desserts & Sweet Treats

Chapter 8

Prelude: Salads

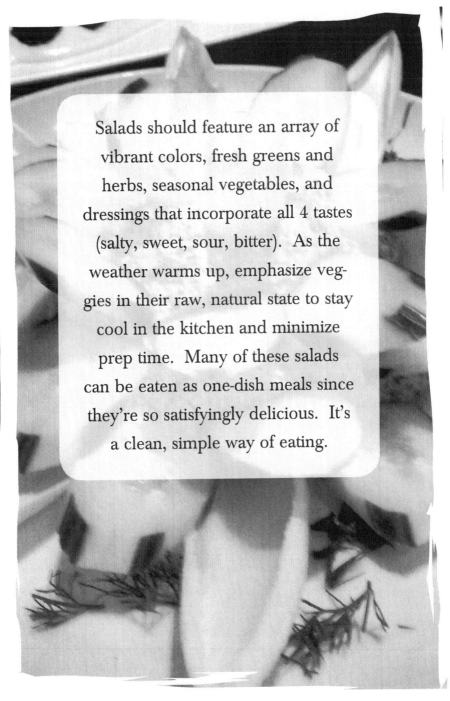

Salads should feature an array of vibrant colors, fresh greens and herbs, seasonal vegetables, and dressings that incorporate all 4 tastes (salty, sweet, sour, bitter). As the weather warms up, emphasize veggies in their raw, natural state to stay cool in the kitchen and minimize prep time. Many of these salads can be eaten as one-dish meals since they're so satisfyingly delicious. It's a clean, simple way of eating.

- Crispy Cruciferous Vegetable Slaw
- Massaged Kale with Granny Smith Apples and Avocado
- Cool Confetti Black Bean and Brown Rice Salad
- "Sea"sar Salad with Pear, Avocado and Tahini Dulse Dressing
- Chickpea "Tuno"
- Tempeh Waldorf Salad
- Shaved Fennel, Jicama and Watercress Salad with Avocado Lime Dressing
- Spring Cleanse Quinoa Salad with Asparagus, Radish, and Pistachios
- Edamame and Black Bean Protein Power Salad
- RAW Curried Cashew Salad in Lettuce Leaf Cups
- Fiesta Quinoa Salad
- Caribbean Jasmine Rice Salad
- Quinoa Tabbouleh

Crispy Cruciferous Vegetable Slaw

(serves 4)

This salad contains bright contrasting colors of green and purple from the cruciferous vegetables broccoli, green cabbage, and purple cabbage, plus the white of cauliflower to ground them. These vegetables are high in phytonutrients with potent anti-cancer properties that help detoxify the body. It's the perfect salad for transitioning from winter to spring as it enhances seasonal cleansing.

Cashew Mayo Ingredients
1 cup cashews (soaked several hours, drained and rinsed)
1 clove garlic
1 tsp apple cider vinegar
1 Tbl lemon juice
1 Tbl Dijon mustard
1 tsp sea salt
1/2 cup water (approx.)

Blend all ingredients in a high-speed blender, gradually adding enough water to make a smooth, thick sauce.

Salad Ingredients
2 1/2 cups broccoli, finely chopped florets and stem
2 1/2 cups cauliflower, finely chopped florets and stem
1 cup red cabbage, shredded
1 Granny Smith apple, finely diced
1/4 cup shallot, finely diced
1/2 cup dried cranberries
1/4 cup pumpkin seeds, soaked, drained and rinsed
1 tsp celery seed

Stir together all ingredients in a medium bowl. Pour Cashew Mayo over vegetable mixture and gently stir to combine. Refrigerate prior to serving.

Massaged Kale with Granny Smith Apples and Avocado

(serves 2-4)

Kale is king when it comes to veggies. It's high in antioxidants, iron, calcium, and vitamins A and C, and it's anti-inflammatory in the body. Its high fiber content aids in digestion and detoxification and helps the absorption of essential nutrients. This salad is a great way to get all of the health benefits kale offers, plus it's satisfying and delicious.

<u>Ingredients</u>
2 Tbl tahini
1-2 tsp tamari
2 Tbl fresh lemon juice
1-2 tsp water
1 large bunch of Lacinato or Russian kale
1 crisp Granny Smith apple, sliced into thin wedges
1 Tbl raw hemp seeds
sea salt

In a large bowl, mix together tahini, tamari, lemon juice and enough water to make a smooth paste. Rinse kale and cut into small pieces, then squeeze and massage kale over a colander to remove excess water. Toss kale in dressing until well coated and season with sea salt. Top with sliced apple and sprinkle with hemp seeds. Add salt to taste.

Cool Confetti Black Bean and Brown Rice Salad

(serves 4-6)

I love serving this salad for a picnic buffet. It's colorful, crunchy, flavorful, and so easy to make. Eat it as a side with your favorite vegan burger, or make it a one-dish meal since it's satisfying on its own. Leftovers keep well for several days in the fridge, so make a double batch and enjoy it all week.

Ingredients

1/4 cup olive oil
juice of 1 lemon (about 2 Tbl)
2-3 cloves crushed garlic
1 seeded and peeled cucumber, finely diced
2-3 green onions, finely cut
1 cup of red cabbage, finely chopped
1 cup carrots, peeled and diced
1 15 oz. can of black beans, drained and rinsed
1 15 oz. can of corn, drained and rinsed
1 cup fresh dill, finely chopped
1 cup cooked brown rice
1 Tbl umeboshi vinegar
1 tsp salt (approx.)

Mix olive oil, lemon juice and garlic together in a large bowl. Add the cucumber, green onions, red cabbage, carrots, beans, corn, and dill and toss with dressing. Carefully fold in brown rice, breaking up clumps as you mix. Add umeboshi vinegar, salt, and your favorite hot sauce (I like Sriracha) to suit your taste. If the salad still needs a little flavor boost, add more umeboshi. Refrigerate at least one hour before serving.

"Sea"sar Salad with Pear, Avocado and Tahini Dulse Dressing

(serves 2-4)

I love a simple yet elegant salad that even non-vegans enjoy. This is one of those "bridge" recipes that helps people seamlessly transition from something they're familiar with to a more compassionate version without feeling like they're missing out on anything.

Ingredients
1 Tbl tahini
1-2 tsp tamari
1-2 Tbl fresh lime juice
1 Tbl dulse granules
1-2 tsp water
1 head of romaine lettuce, cut into bite-sized pieces
1 ripe pear, sliced
1 avocado, sliced
sea salt
fresh ground black pepper

In a large bowl, mix together tahini, tamari, lime juice, dulse granules, and enough water to make a thick paste. Toss lettuce in dressing until well coated, then top with pear and avocado and sprinkle with salt and fresh ground pepper.

Chickpea "Tuno"

(serves 4)

This is sure to be a guaranteed "go to" favorite in your family. Whenever I host a potluck or picnic, everyone begs me to serve it. The taste is reminiscent of the real thing, but no tunas were harmed in the making.

Ingredients
1 15-ounce can chickpeas, drained and rinsed
1/2 cup chopped celery, from about one rib
1/4 cup red onion, diced
1/4 cup pickle, diced finely (or pickle relish)
1 Tbl dulse granules
1/2 cup vegan mayo
1 Tbl Dijon mustard
1 Tbl lemon juice
1-2 tsp apple cider vinegar
2 tsp garlic powder
1/2 tsp sea salt (to taste)

In a large bowl, mash chickpeas with a potato masher until crumbly but still have some large pieces. (For a finer texture, briefly pulse in food processor.) Toss with celery, red onion, chopped pickle and dulse powder. Add remaining ingredients and stir to combine.

Tempeh Waldorf Salad

(serves 4)

I like the sweet and savory combo of this salad. Substituting tempeh is an easy way to veganize the traditional recipe which many of us remember as a sandwich filling on white bread and packing it into our lunchbox as we headed off to school. Fortunately, this version's much healthier.

<u>Ingredients</u>
8 ounces tempeh (Lightlife), cut into cubes
1/2 cup vegan mayonnaise
1 Tbl Dijon mustard
1 Tbl fresh squeezed lemon juice
1/4 tsp garlic powder
1/4 tsp sea salt
1 stalk celery, diced fine
1/4 cup red onion, diced fine
1/2 cup Granny Smith apple, diced fine
1/2 cup chopped walnuts
1/2 cup red seedless grapes, sliced in half

Bring a large pot of water to a boil. Add tempeh cubes and boil 5 minutes, then drain and rinse with cold water until cool to the touch. Squeeze tempeh cubes over colander to remove excess water and set aside. In a large mixing bowl, whisk together vegan mayonnaise, mustard, lemon juice, garlic powder, and sea salt. Combine with crumbled tempeh and remaining ingredients, mixing lightly but well.

Shaved Fennel, Jicama and Watercress Salad with Avocado Lime Dressing

(serves 2-4)

This is a great salad for the end of winter/early spring when fresh greens like watercress are beginning to come into season. Be prepared for lots of crunch.

Dressing Ingredients
half an avocado
1 Tbl brown rice vinegar
1/4 cup fresh squeezed orange juice (juice of ½ an orange)
1 Tbl lime juice
1/4 tsp sea salt
1 Tbl agave syrup
1 clove garlic
water

Salad Ingredients
1 cup jicama, peeled and cut into matchsticks
1 cup fennel, shaved into thin strips
1 small bunch of watercress or baby greens
1/2 an orange, peeled into slices
1/4 cup unsalted raw cashews, chopped coarsely
cilantro

Combine all dressing ingredients in a blender and puree, gradually adding enough water to make the dressing smooth and creamy. Reserve half of the dressing. Cut up vegetables and set aside a handful of jicama and fennel for garnish. Toss remaining vegetables in bowl with dressing. Arrange a small bunch of watercress or baby greens on plate and top with dressed jicama and fennel. Arrange sliced orange sections either on top or along the sides. Sprinkle reserved jicama, fennel and chopped cashews over the top, then garnish with a few cilantro leaves.

Spring Cleanse Quinoa Salad with Asparagus, Radish, and Pistachios

(serves 4)

I like making this salad when the wild chives start popping up in the yard after the snow melts because it really fills me with positive spring energy. If you can find these, use them. Otherwise you can simply substitute scallions.

Ingredients

1 cup asparagus, cut on the diagonal into 1-inch pieces
2 Tbl olive oil
1 Tbl Dijon mustard
1 1/2 Tbl fresh lemon juice
1-2 tsp agave syrup
1/2 tsp sea salt
1/2 cup radish, cut into matchsticks
2 Tbl minced shallots
2 Tbl fresh chopped scallion or wild chives
2 cups cooked quinoa
2 Tbl chopped pistachios

Bring a large pot of water to boil. Add asparagus and let blanch for one minute. Drain asparagus into a colander and immediately rinse with cold water. In a large bowl, whisk together olive oil, Dijon mustard, lemon juice, agave syrup and sea salt. Toss with asparagus, radish, shallots, and scallion, then gently stir in quinoa. Top with chopped pistachios.

EZPZ Tip

For perfectly fluffy quinoa, start with 1 cup of quinoa (rinsed and drained) and 1 1/2 cups water in a sauce pot. Cover pot, bring to a boil, then reduce heat to low. Cook for 15 minutes, then remove saucepan from heat and let sit for 5 minutes. Uncover and fluff gently. Using this method, 1 cup of raw quinoa yields about 1 1/2 to 2 cups cooked.

Edamame Black Bean Super Protein Power Salad

(serves 2-4)

Whether you're looking for a quick supper that works great as lunch leftovers or an easy dish to bring to a potluck, this is the perfect recipe. The ingredient list is short and sweet, yet the finished product packs a punch of flavor, and it looks super pretty, too.

Ingredients
2 Tbl olive oil
1 Tbl tahini
1 Tbl Dijon mustard
1 Tbl lemon juice
1 tsp agave syrup
1 tsp apple cider vinegar
1/4 tsp sea salt
1 10 oz. bag frozen shelled edamame, thawed
1 15 oz. can black beans, drained and rinsed
1 10 oz. bag frozen corn, thawed
1/2 cup red onion, diced to the size of a corn kernel
1 red pepper, diced to the size of a corn kernel
2 cloves garlic, minced

In a large bowl, whisk together olive oil, tahini, mustard, lemon juice, agave, apple cider vinegar, and sea salt to make a smooth and creamy paste. Stir in remaining ingredients and season to taste.

RAW Curried Cashew Salad in Lettuce Leaf Cups

(serves 2-4)
If you crave curry like I do but don't want to wait for a big pot of it to simmer on the stove, you'll want to make this recipe.

Ingredients
1 1/2 cups chopped cashews (soaked several hours, drained and rinsed)
2 carrots, cut into quarter moons
2 stalks celery, finely diced
1 green onion, finely diced
Handful of chopped fresh oregano
1 head of baby bib lettuce

Dressing Ingredients
1 heaping Tbl almond butter
Juice of 1/2 a lemon (about 2 Tbl)
1/2 tsp curry powder
1/4 tsp turmeric
1/8 tsp sea salt
Water

Combine cashews, carrots, celery, green onion and oregano together in a bowl. In a separate bowl, mix together ingredients for dressing and add enough water to make a thick sauce. Drizzle dressing over other ingredients and stir to combine. Line a soup bowl with baby bib lettuce leaves. Fill with a generous scoop of Curried Cashew Salad.

Fiesta Quinoa Salad
(serves 4)

This summery salad is as pretty as it is delicious. Use fresh corn when it's in season to really boost the sweet and spicy flavor contrast.

Dressing Ingredients
2 Tbl fresh squeezed lime juice
2 tsp apple cider vinegar
1-2 tsp agave syrup
1 Tbl olive oil
1 clove garlic, minced fine
2 tsp cumin
2 tsp chili powder
1/4 tsp powdered chipotle pepper
1/2 tsp sea salt

Salad Ingredients
2 cups cooked quinoa
1 cup fresh corn
pinch of sea salt
1 15 oz. can black beans (rinsed and drained)
1/2 cup finely diced red pepper
1/2 cup finely diced green pepper
2-3 scallions, diced
1/4 cup cilantro leaves

Whisk the dressing ingredients together in a large bowl until well combined. Gently fold in the salad ingredients until dressing is evenly distributed.

Caribbean Jasmine Rice Salad

(serves 2-4)
This is a sweet and slightly spicy salad that pairs well with Jerk Tempeh.

Ingredients
1 cup jasmine rice
3/4 cup dried coconut
2 cups of water
1 cup fresh chopped pineapple (or 8 oz. canned chunk)
1/2 cup red bell pepper, diced
1 Tbl jalapeño pepper, diced
3 scallions, finely diced
1/2 cup roughly chopped cashews
1/4 tsp red pepper flakes
1/8 tsp cumin
1/8 tsp paprika
1/4 tsp salt
2 Tbl lime juice
2 Tbl olive oil

Bring water, rice and coconut to boil in a covered pot. Lower heat and simmer 15 minutes. Remove lid and check to see that all of the water has been absorbed and rice is not sticking. Remove from heat and gently fluff cooked rice with a fork. Set aside rice to cool. Meanwhile, combine remaining ingredients in a large bowl, reserving about 1/4 cup of cashews and 1/4 cup of diced scallions for garnish. Gently stir in cooled rice and top with reserved scallions and cashews.

EZPZ Tip
If you'd like to substitute whole grain brown rice for jasmine rice in this recipe, cook rice for about 35-40 minutes.

Quinoa Tabbouleh
(serves 2-4)

This is a gluten-free twist on tabbouleh that is traditionally made with bulgur wheat. Since quinoa is a seed instead of a grain, it's lighter and fluffier and loaded with protein and lower in carbohydrates.

Ingredients
1 cup cooked quinoa
1 bunch curly parsley, chopped fine
1 bunch fresh mint, chopped fine
1 cucumber, peeled, seeded and cut into medium dice
1/2 red onion, finely diced
2 tomatoes, diced
1 green onion, diced
2 cloves garlic, minced or pressed through garlic press
1/4 cup extra virgin olive oil
Juice of 1 lemon
Sea salt to taste
Black pepper to taste

In a large bowl, toss together ingredients for tabbouleh and season with sea salt and pepper. Refrigerate before serving.

Chapter 9

Prelude: Soups

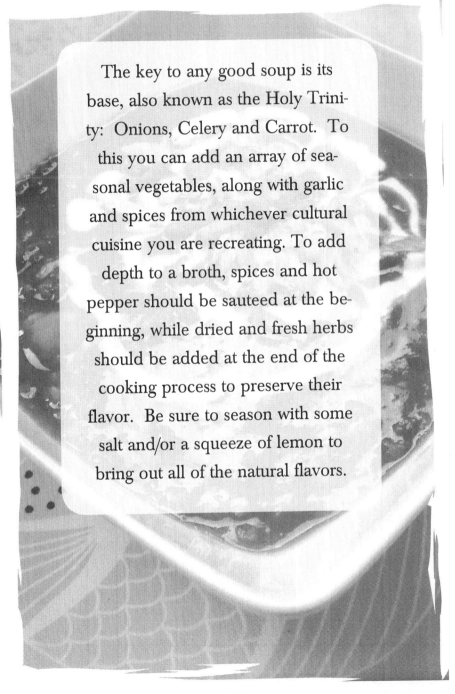

The key to any good soup is its base, also known as the Holy Trinity: Onions, Celery and Carrot. To this you can add an array of seasonal vegetables, along with garlic and spices from whichever cultural cuisine you are recreating. To add depth to a broth, spices and hot pepper should be sauteed at the beginning, while dried and fresh herbs should be added at the end of the cooking process to preserve their flavor. Be sure to season with some salt and/or a squeeze of lemon to bring out all of the natural flavors.

- Velvety Vegan Vichyssoise
- Gingered Butternut Bisque
- Red Lentil and Jasmine Rice Coconut Curry
- French Lentils with Spinach and Lemon
- Tuscan White Bean and Garlic Greens Soup
- Three-Bean Cha Cha Cha Chili
- Smoked Paprika Green and Yellow Split Pea Soup
- Warm Summer Evening Gazpacho Soup
- Cool as a Cucumber Soup
- Super Green Power Soup
- Minted Spring Vegetable Bisque
- African Sweet Potato and Peanut Stew
- Three Sisters Stew

Velvety Vegan Vichyssoise with Herb Oil

(serves 4)

If mashed potatoes make you smile, this recipe will have you swooning.

Vichyssoise

3-4 cups of peeled, diced potatoes (approx 8 potatoes)
3 cups of leeks, white part only, cut into half moons
8 cups of water
1 Tbl sea salt
1/2 to 1 cup of vanilla rice milk
2-3 Tbl vegan margarine
2-3 Tbl fresh chopped chives or scallions

Bring pot of water to a boil then simmer potatoes and leeks until tender. Drain water, then return potatoes and leeks to the pot. Mash until semi-smooth, yet still retaining some chunks. Add salt and margarine, then set aside to cool. Reheat to a simmer just prior to serving and stir in rice milk to form a soup consistency. Garnish with fresh chopped chives and herb oil.

Herb Oil

1/2 cup extra virgin olive oil
1 cup fresh parsley leaves (or substitute any fresh, seasonal herb such as dill)
1/2 tsp dried Italian seasoning
1 Tbl lemon juice
1 clove garlic
salt and pepper

Puree ingredients in a blender until herb leaves are finely chopped. Pour mixture into squeeze bottle. Drizzle a swirl of herb oil over the top of the Vichyssoise.

EZPZ Tip
Dress up this recipe with a garnish of fresh chives and/or chive blossoms when they're in season in the early spring.

Gingered Butternut Bisque

(serves 4)

This is a lovely soup for the autumn harvest table. I like serving it as a first course for Thanksliving Dinner garnished with Spiced Pepitas. Why not make it a part of your holiday tradition?

<u>Ingredients</u>
1 Tbl olive oil
1 cup yellow onion, chopped
1 clove garlic, minced
1-inch piece of fresh ginger, minced
1 cup garnet yam, peeled and cut into 2-inch cubes
2 large carrots, peeled and cut into 2-inch pieces
1 large parsnip, peeled and cut into 2-inch pieces
1 cup butternut squash, peeled and cut into 2-inch cubes
2 cups rice milk
1 tsp sea salt
2 Tbl mellow white miso dissolved in 1/4 cup rice milk
1 scallion, sliced fine
pinch of cayenne

In a large pot, sauté onion, garlic and ginger in olive oil until translucent. Add yam, carrots, parsnip and squash and 2 cups of water and bring to a boil. Lower heat and simmer approximately 15-20 minutes, or until vegetables are fork-tender. Turn off heat and let cool 10-15 minutes. Place cooled vegetables and miso in blender and puree with enough rice milk to make mixture smooth and creamy. Season with sea salt. If soup is too thick, add more rice milk. Returned pureed soup to pot and simmer over low heat before serving. Garnish with fresh scallions and a tiny pinch of cayenne pepper.

Red Lentil and Jasmine Rice Coconut Curry

(serves 4)

On a cold and dreary day, this is a satisfying soup that comes together quickly. The flavors will perk you up, and the spices combined with ginger, garlic and lemon will boost your immune system. At the first sign of a cold, whip up a big pot and you'll feel healthy in no time.

<u>Ingredients</u>
1 onion, diced
1 clove garlic, minced
2-inch slice of fresh ginger, minced
1 cup red lentils
1/2 cup jasmine rice
6 cups water
1 tsp turmeric
2 tsp curry powder
1/2 cup coconut milk (from can)
1 tsp sea salt
juice of 1 lemon (about 2-3 Tbl)
chopped cilantro for garnish (optional)

Place onion, garlic, ginger, lentils, rice, turmeric, curry powder, and water in a large sauce pot, cover, and bring to a boil. Lower heat and simmer gently for 20 - 30 minutes until the lentils are soft and rice is cooked. You may need to adjust the water and amount of cooking time depending on the consistency you prefer. Once the correct consistency is achieved, season with sea salt, add the fresh lemon juice and coconut milk, and stir in the cilantro just before serving.

EZPZ Tip
Adding a squeeze of lemon at the end of cooking your soup will brighten up the flavors.

French Lentils with Spinach and Lemon

(serves 4-6)

This is a spicy twist on a basic lentil recipe, yet it's not too overpowering. I like to make a big pot at the beginning of the week and serve it over rice or pasta for a quick and easy meal.

<u>Soup Ingredients</u>
2 Tbl olive oil
1 cup onion, diced
1 celery stalk, diced
1 carrot, diced into quarter moons
2 cups French lentils
2 medium potatoes, washed, peeled, and cut into 1 cubes
8 cups water
2 tsp sea salt
1 pound baby spinach

<u>Spice Ingredients</u>
2 Tbl olive oil
5 cloves garlic, minced
1 tsp ground coriander
1 tsp cumin seeds
3/4 cup chopped fresh cilantro
3-4 tbsp fresh lemon juice
thin slices of lemon, for garnish

Heat 2 tablespoons of olive oil in a large soup pan over medium-high heat. Add the onion, celery, and carrot and cook several minutes, or until soft. Add the lentils, potatoes, and the water, bring to a boil, then cover, turn the heat to low, and simmer for about 35-45 minutes, stirring occasionally. When lentils have softened, stir in the sea salt and spinach and cook for about 10 minutes, or until spinach has wilted.

In a separate skillet, heat 2 tablespoons of olive oil on medium heat. Add the garlic, coriander, cumin, and coriander and saute for about 3 minutes. Stir in the fresh cilantro and sauté until just wilted. Combine with the pot of lentils along with the fresh squeezed lemon juice, adding more water if it seems too thick. Season with salt and lemon juice, if necessary, and serve garnished with thin slices of lemon and fresh cilantro.

Tuscan White Beans and Garlic Greens Soup

(serves 4)
When it's cold outside and you're looking for something to warm you up quickly, this is the soup to make.

<u>Soup Ingredients</u>
1 Tbl olive oil
1 onion, diced
2-3 cloves garlic, minced
6 cups water
2 carrots, peeled and diced
2 medium red potatoes, peeled and cut into 1/2 in. cubes
15 oz. can of cannelini beans, drained and rinsed
1/2 cup tomato paste mixed with a few tablespoons of water
1 tsp dried basil
1 Tbl dried oregano
1 tsp sea salt

<u>Topping Ingredients</u>
2 Tbl toasted pine nuts
1-2 Tbl olive oil
1-2 cloves garlic, minced
large bunch shredded kale, collard, Swiss chard or spinach
sea salt, fresh crushed black pepper to taste

In a large soup pot, sauté onion and garlic in olive oil until translucent. Add water, carrots and potatoes and bring to a boil. Lower heat and simmer covered for 15-20 minutes, or until potatoes are soft. Add beans, tomato paste, herbs and salt. In a separate pan, heat pine nuts until fragrant and lightly browned, then set aside. Heat olive oil and garlic until fragrant. Stir in greens, sprinkle with salt, and cook several minutes or until wilted. Ladle soup into bowls and top with sauteed greens and toasted pine nuts. Season with salt and pepper.

Three Bean Cha Cha Cha Chili

(serves 2-4)

Everybody needs a good, reliable chili recipe and this one is a favorite. I love the rich spices of adobo and fire-roasted tomatoes which add depth to the finished dish.

Ingredients

1 Tbl olive oil
1 small yellow onion, diced
1 green pepper, diced
2 garlic cloves, minced
2 tsp chili powder
1 Tbl cumin
1/4 tsp red pepper flakes (optional)
2 15 oz. cans of fire-roasted tomatoes in adobo (Muir Glen brand)
1 15 oz. can of black beans, drained and rinsed
1 15 oz. can of red kidney beans, drained and rinsed
1 15 oz. can of pinto beans, drained and rinsed
1/2 tsp sea salt

In a medium pan, sauté onion and green pepper in oil until soft, stirring frequently, for about 10 minutes. Stir in garlic, chili powder, cumin, and red pepper flakes and let cook until fragrant, about 30 seconds. Add tomatoes and beans and cook until tomatoes soften, about 10 minutes. Season with salt.

Smoked Paprika Green and Yellow Split Pea Soup

(serves 2-4)

The smokiness of paprika and chipotle are perfect stand-ins for the traditional ham hock base of this soup, which you will never miss. I love it with a dollop of cashew sour creme swirled on top.

Ingredients

1/2 cup green split peas
1/2 cup yellow split peas
2 Tbl olive oil
1 cup yellow onion, diced
2 stalks celery, diced (approx. 1/2 cup)
1 large carrot, peeled and diced (approx. 1 cup)
4 cloves garlic, minced through garlic press
1 tsp smoked paprika
1/2 tsp chipotle powder
1 large Russet potato, peeled and cut into 1-inch dice
5 cups water
1 tsp sea salt
1 Tbl fresh lemon juice
2 scallion, diced

Rinse split peas in a colander and set aside to drain. In a large pot, saute onion, celery, and carrots in olive oil on medium heat for 5-10 minutes, or until lightly browned. Add garlic, paprika, and chipotle and saute one minute. Add split peas, potato and water, then cover pot and bring to a boil. Lower heat and simmer 1 hour or until split peas are soft, stirring occasionally. If soup is too thick, add a little more water. Stir in fresh lemon juice and garnish with chopped scallion.

Warm Summer Evening Gazpacho Soup

(serves 4)

When it's too hot to heat up the kitchen and I'm not in the mood for a salad, this is my favorite "go to" soup. You'll love the refreshing flavors and be surprised by the hardiness.

Ingredients

1 medium cucumber, peeled, seeded, and diced
1 zucchini, diced
1 small green bell pepper, seeded and diced
1/2 cup red onion, diced
1 stalk of celery, diced
1 avocado, diced
2-3 cloves garlic, minced
1-2 Tbl fresh lemon juice
2 Tbl olive oil
1/2 tsp cumin
1/4 tsp sea salt, to taste
1 32 oz. bottle of organic tomato juice (I like Knudsen original)

Dice cucumber, zucchini, green pepper, red onion, celery, and avocado, reserving about a 1/4 cup of each for garnish. Place diced vegetables, garlic, lemon juice, and olive oil in food processor and blend until almost pureed, leaving some texture. Add tomato juice, cumin and sea salt and pulse to combine. Garnish with reserved veggies.

Cool as a Cucumber Soup

(serves 4)
Cucumbers really do have a cooling effect on the body, plus they're loaded with water, so they help prevent dehydration during the heat of summer. This is a quick recipe that works well for a light lunch.

Ingredients
3-4 medium cucumbers, peeled, seeded, and roughly diced
2 Tbl olive oil
2 Tbl rice vinegar
handful fresh dill, chopped
Romaine lettuce, leaves roughly chopped handful fresh parsley, chopped
1 avocado, diced
1-2 cloves garlic
juice of half a lime (about 1 Tbl)
1/4 tsp sea salt
2 Tbl capers
1 cup water

Reserve 1/2 cup of thinly sliced cucumber rounds, place into a large bowl, and toss with a drizzle of olive oil, splash of vinegar, pinch of sea salt and 1 Tbl chopped fresh dill. In a blender, puree remaining cucumbers, lettuce, parsley, avocado, garlic, lime juice, vinegar, olive oil, salt, capers, and water until smooth. Season with additional salt. Transfer to a large bowl and refrigerate. Divide soup among 4 bowls, lay cucumber slices over soup and garnish with dill sprig.

Super Green Power Soup

(serves 4)

This soup is like a super smooth, multicultural green gazpacho that incorporates the salty-sweetness of mellow white miso and creamy richness of tahini. The flavors meld together in perfect harmony.

Ingredients
2 small zucchinis, chopped
1/2 cup of water, plus about ½ cup to thin
1 ripe medium sized tomato, chopped
1 celery stalk, chopped
1 green onion, chopped
1 Tbl lemon juice
2-3 tsp mellow white miso
Pinch of sea salt
1 cup of baby spinach
10 basil leaves, chopped
1 ripe avocado
1 Tbl tahini
1 tsp sesame seeds

In a blender, puree zucchinis, ½ cup of water, tomato, celery, green onion, lemon juice, miso and sea salt until smooth. Add the spinach and basil and blend again. Add the avocado and tahini and briefly puree with enough water until a smooth consistency is achieved. Garnish with sesame seeds.

Minted Spring Vegetable Bisque

(serves 2-4)

I look forward to the first signs of spring every year, and this soup just gets me in the mood for that change of season. This is the perfect starter to celebrate St. Patrick's Day or the Vernal Equinox.

Ingredients

approx. 2 cups asparagus, diced, woody ends removed
approx. 2 cups snap peas
1-2 cups soy milk or rice milk
1 large Russet potato, peeled and diced
1 cup water
1 leek, cut thinly and rinsed thoroughly
1-2 cloves garlic
olive oil
sea salt
2 Tbl fresh mint, chopped fine

Blanch snap peas in boiling water for about 2 minutes, then rinse in cold water. Blanch asparagus for about 1 minute, then rinse in cold water. Set both aside, reserving a few asparagus tips for garnish. In a large pot, sauté leek and garlic in olive oil until soft. Add potatoes, 1 cup of water and 1 cup of rice milk and bring to a boil. Let cook for 10-12 minutes, or until soft. Let cool, then gradually pour mixture along with asparagus and snap peas into a blender. Puree until smooth. You may need to do this in several batches, adding more rice milk as necessary to get the right consistency.

Pour mixture back into pot then heat for about 10 minutes, skimming foam off the top if necessary. Add chopped mint just before serving.

African Sweet Potato and Peanut Stew

(serves 4)

This is one of those hearty soups you'll want to eat whenever the weather turns chilly. There is a perfect balance of sweet, savory, spicy, and sour which leave you feeling satisfied, plus the added crunch of peanuts make each delicious bite last that much longer.

Ingredients

1 sweet potato, peeled, cut into 1-inch cubes
1-2 Tbl olive oil
1 small onion, diced
1 green pepper, diced
1 clove garlic, minced
2 carrots, peeled and cut into thin rounds
1 cup green beans, ends trimmed and cut into 1-inch pieces
1-inch piece of fresh ginger, minced
1 Tbl cumin
1-2 tsp cinnamon
pinch of cayenne (optional)
1 tsp sea salt
1 15 oz. can of crushed tomatoes

2 Tbl peanut butter mixed with ¼ cup of water
1 cup canned coconut milk
3 limes, juice of 2 limes (approx. 2 Tbl) and reserve 1 lime for garnish
1-2 Tbl agave syrup
1 cup of frozen peas
1/2 cup chopped peanuts
2-3 green onions, chopped

Bring a large pot of water to a boil and add sweet potatoes, cooking about 10-12 minutes, or until fork tender. Set aside. Meanwhile, in a large pot, sauté onion and green pepper in olive oil until soft. Add carrot, green beans, and a pinch of sea salt and cook several minutes or until soft. Stir in garlic, ginger, cumin, cinnamon, cayenne, and salt and cook until fragrant (1-2 minutes). Add crushed tomatoes and pre-cooked sweet potatoes and cook several minutes. Carefully stir in peanut butter and water mixture, coconut milk, lime juice and agave syrup. Taste for seasoning, then add peas and chopped peanuts. Simmer 10-15 minutes and season with salt before serving. Reserve 1 lime to cut into 4 wedges for garnish.

Three Sisters Stew

(serves 4)

As summer comes to an end and the cool weather approaches, this is the perfect recipe for incorporating the three main agricultural crops of the late season harvest: corn, beans, and squash. These three vegetables are considered "3 sisters" because Native Americans interplanted them for their harmonious growth habits. The corn grows tall and serves as support for climbing runner beans, while squash vines shade their feet and crowd out weeds along the ground. The three vegetables also share complimentary flavors of savory and sweet and form a complete protein when consumed together. Served on top of creamy polenta (made from corn meal) and garnished with spicy toasted pumpkin seeds (also in the squash family), the three sisters make a delicious seasonal treat.

Ingredients
2-3 Tbl olive oil
1 cup onion, diced
2 cups summer squash, cut into quarter moons
2 cups green beans, trimmed and cut into 1-inch pieces
2-3 cloves garlic, minced
1/4 tsp red pepper flakes
1-2 tsp cumin
1-2 tsp dried oregano
1 lb. diced tomatoes (or 1 28 oz. can)
1/4 cup tomato paste
1 cup corn
1 15 oz. can pinto beans, drained and rinsed
1/2 tsp sea salt
fresh black pepper

In a large sauce pot, sauté onion in olive oil until it sweats and is starting to brown, about 5 minutes. Add summer squash and green beans and cook until fork tender, about 5 minutes. Add garlic, red pepper flakes, cumin and oregano and heat for about a minute until fragrant. Stir in diced tomatoes, tomato paste, corn, and pinto beans and heat for 10-15 minutes, or until sauce thickens. Season with salt and pepper.

Chapter 10

Prelude: Starters

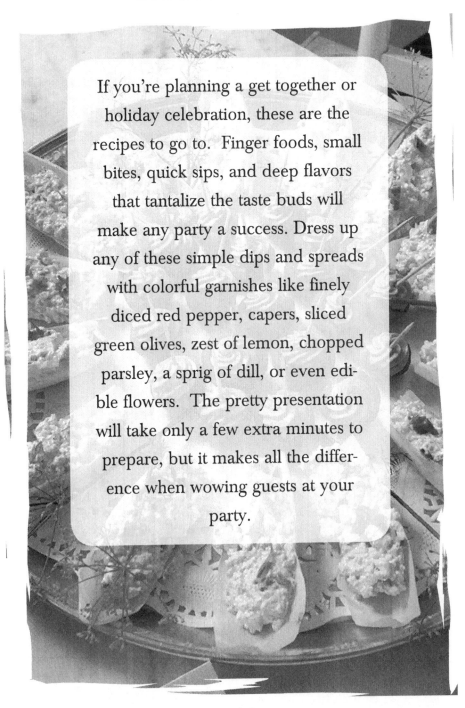

If you're planning a get together or holiday celebration, these are the recipes to go to. Finger foods, small bites, quick sips, and deep flavors that tantalize the taste buds will make any party a success. Dress up any of these simple dips and spreads with colorful garnishes like finely diced red pepper, capers, sliced green olives, zest of lemon, chopped parsley, a sprig of dill, or even edible flowers. The pretty presentation will take only a few extra minutes to prepare, but it makes all the difference when wowing guests at your party.

- Cashew Cream Cheese
- Sun-dried Tomato Tapenade
- Vegan Caviar (Olive Tapenade)
- Cannelini Artichoke Dip
- Tangy Black Bean Hummus
- Holiday Spinach Dip
- Eggplant Caponata
- Eggless Egg Salad on Cucumber Rounds
- Mini Mediterranean Quiches
- Strawberry Salsa with Cilantro Vinaigrette
- Summer Solstice Cherry and Peach Compote
- Equinox Elixir

Cashew Cream Cheese

This versatile recipe can be used as a dip for crudites, a spread on crackers, or a stuffing for veggies. My favorite way to serve it for a party hors d'oeuvre is piped from a pastry bag onto endive leaves, then topped with a spoonful of Sun-dried Tomato Tapenade. It makes a colorful, festive presentation that is tantalizingly tasty.

Ingredients
1 cup cashews (soaked several hours, drained and rinsed)
1 clove garlic
2 Tbl lemon juice
1 tsp apple cider vinegar
1-2 Tbl nutritional yeast
1/4 tsp sea salt
Enough water to bring to creamy consistency (approx. 1/4 cup)

In a food processor, puree cashews and garlic with enough water to bring to a smooth consistency. Add remaining ingredients and blend until creamy.

EZPZ Tip
Vary this recipe by adding aromatic herbs like fresh rosemary or dill, or spice it up with a sprinkle of turmeric and curry powder.

Sun-dried Tomato Tapenade

I love this served with gluten-free toast points or as a companion to cashew cream cheese in endive leaves for a pretty hors d'oeuvre. It's also delicious on top of spiralized zucchini for a healthy raw lunch.

<u>Ingredients</u>
8 sun-dried tomatoes
4 campari tomatoes, seeded and chopped
1/4 cup kalamata olives
2 cloves garlic, minced
2 Tbl chopped fresh parsley
1/4 cup chopped fresh basil
Sea salt to taste
2 Tbl extra virgin olive oil (optional)

In a food processor, pulse sun-dried tomatoes 3-4 times, or until roughly chopped. Add tomatoes, olives and garlic and pulse 5-6 times in a food processor or until coarsely chopped. Add remaining ingredients and pulse 1-2 times to combine. .

Vegan Caviar (Olive Tapenade)

As an alternative to sun-dried tomato, this is another tapenade that works well on crostini or crackers. Alternatively, it can be tossed with pasta and baby spinach for a quick and flavorful meal.

Ingredients
1/4 cup walnuts
2-3 Tbl olive oil
2 cloves of garlic (optional)
3/4 cup kalamata olives
1/4 cup green olives
2 Tbl capers
3 Tbl chopped fresh parsley
1/4 tsp sea salt
crushed black pepper (optional)

Pulse walnuts in food processor until roughly chopped. Combine with remaining ingredients and pulse until a paste is formed, leaving some texture. Refrigerate before serving.

Cannelini Artichoke Dip

This is another versatile recipe that can be used as a dip for raw veggies or spread on crostini. You may even want to try it on mini finger sandwiches topped with a thinly sliced cucumber and radish round.

Ingredients

1 5 oz. jar of artichoke hearts, drained
1 15 oz. can of cannelini beans, drained and rinsed
1 clove garlic
1 green onion
1 Tbl nutritional yeast
juice of half a lemon (about 2 Tbl)
2 Tbl olive oil
1/2 tsp sea salt, to taste
black pepper to taste
2 tsp capers
sprinkle of paprika

Combine all ingredients except capers and paprika in a food processor and puree until smooth. If needed, add several tablespoons of water to get to the right consistency. Pulse capers in at the end and reserve a few for garnish. Top dip with remaining capers, a sprinkle of paprika and a drizzle of olive oil.

Tangy Black Bean Hummus

Serve as a dip with corn chips. This also makes a great filling for burritos.

<u>Ingredients</u>
1 medium tomato
1-2 scallions
1 jalapeño pepper
1 ripe avocado
15 oz. can of black beans, drained and rinsed
Juice from 1/2 a lemon
1-2 cloves of garlic, crushed
1 tsp chili powder
1/4 cup rice milk
1/4 tsp sea salt
Chopped fresh cilantro (optional)

Dice tomato, scallions, pepper and avocado. Place in a food processor with black beans, lemon juice, garlic, chili powder, rice milk, and sea salt. Puree until well mixed and creamy, then top with fresh cilantro.

Holiday Spinach Dip
Another great dip for raw vegetable crudites, chips, or crackers.

Ingredients
10 oz. package of frozen chopped spinach, thawed and squeezed dry
2 scallions, coarsely chopped
1 clove garlic, pressed
4 oz. silken tofu
2 Tbl lemon juice
2 Tbl soy sauce
2 Tbl vegan mayonnaise
dash of Tabasco or Sriracha

Combine all ingredients except spinach in a food processor and puree until smooth. Pour into bowl and stir in spinach.

Eggless Egg Salad

I like using this recipe to make a pretty presentation for parties by placing a scoop of this salad on cucumber rounds or in endive leaves and topping with a sprinkling of finely sliced green onion. Alternatively, it can be used more traditionally as a super yummy sandwich spread.

Ingredients
1/4 cup green onion, finely sliced
2 stalks celery, finely diced
1 dill pickle, finely diced
1 package of extra firm tofu, drained
1/2 tsp turmeric
1/2 tsp sea salt
1/2 cup vegan mayonnaise
1 Tbl Dijon mustard
1 tsp apple cider vinegar

Place green onion, celery, and pickle in a large bowl. Crumble tofu into small chunks on top of veggies. Sprinkle with turmeric and sea salt. Gently stir in vegan mayonnaise, Dijon mustard and apple cider vinegar until color and texture resemble chopped eggs. Add more turmeric if it needs to be more yellow, but be careful not to add too much or it will turn a day-glo yellow hue. Season with salt to taste.

Mini Mediterranean Quiches

(makes 6)

These can be made as cute little hors d'oeuvres for a festive holiday party or in one 8" tart pan for a brunch buffet. Either way, the end result is heavenly deliciousness.

Crust Ingredients
1/2 cup almonds, ground into fine meal
1/2 cup gluten-free flour
2 Tbl cornstarch
1/2 tsp xanthan gum
1/4 tsp sea salt
1/4 cup olive oil
1-2 Tbl water

Filling Ingredients
1/2 cup cashews, soaked in water several hours, drained and rinsed
1/4 cup water
2 Tbl nutritional yeast
1/2 tsp sea salt
1 clove garlic
1 Tbl lemon juice
1/2 cup finely diced onion
8 sun-dried tomatoes, sliced
1 packed cup chopped kale

Preheat oven to 400 degrees and line muffin tins with 6 paper muffin cups. Pulse crust ingredients together in a food processor, gradually adding enough water until dough starts to clump together. Carefully remove dough from food processor and place in a bowl, then chill in the refrigerator for half an hour. Meanwhile, prepare filling ingredients by placing soaked cashews, water, nutritional yeast, sea salt, garlic and lemon in food processor and blend until smooth. Add diced onion, sun-dried tomatoes and chopped kale and pulse together several times until blended but not pureed. Remove dough from refrigerator and separate into 6 balls. Carefully press each dough ball into muffin cups, creating a well in the center. The dough should be about 1/4 inch thick on bottom and sides. Prebake mini quiches for 5-10 minutes, or until crust is lightly golden. Remove from oven, then spoon filling into each dough-lined mini quiche cup. Bake mini quiches 20-25 minutes, or until crust is golden brown. Let cool before serving.

Strawberry Salsa with Cilantro Vinaigrette

When strawberries are in season and you want to try something different, this is the recipe to go for. You'll enjoy the savory/sweet combination that pairs well with spicy black bean dip. But PLEASE, do NOT make this in the middle of winter unless you want a pile of pale and flavorless semi-berries.

Ingredients

1 cup chopped strawberries
1 cup chopped tomato
1 avocado, diced small
1 clove garlic, minced fine
4 tablespoons chopped cilantro
1 Tbl olive oil
1-2 Tbl fresh lime juice
1/4 tsp cumin
1/2 teaspoon sea salt

Gently mix ingredients together in a bowl.

Summer Solstice Cherry and Peach Compote

Rainier cherries are the pretty golden hued robs with a blush of pink. They have a luscious sweet taste and pair nicely with peaches which tend to be in season around the same time.

Ingredients
1 cup Rainier cherries
3 fresh peaches
juice of 1 orange (about ¼ cup)
1/8 tsp cinnamon
pinch of sea salt
1 Tbl chopped fresh mint

Reserve 2-4 cherries, cut in half for garnish. In a food processor, pulse together cherries, peaches, and orange juice until well chopped and mixed. Add cinnamon, sea salt and fresh mint and pulse 2-3 times just to combine. Garnish with cherry halves and fresh mint.

Equinox Elixir

This refreshing smoothie is the perfect way to toast the change of seasons. Its luscious green color will have you thinking Spring in no time.

Ingredients
1 ripe banana
1 ripe pear
1 cup pineapple
1/2 cup rice, hemp, or almond milk
2 leaves of kale, collard greens or spinach
enough water to puree everything smoooooth

Combine all of the above ingredients in a high-speed blender. You may need to chop the greens first so that they blend in fully.

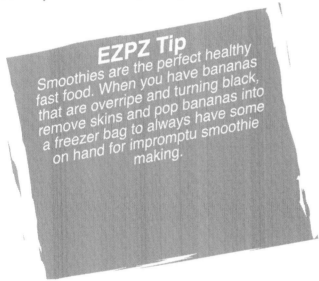

EZPZ Tip
Smoothies are the perfect healthy fast food. When you have bananas that are overripe and turning black, remove skins and pop bananas into a freezer bag to always have some on hand for impromptu smoothie making.

Chapter 11

Verse: On the Side

There's the mistaken assumption that when you take the meat out of your diet, all that's left are the sides. Another way of looking at it is that without the meat you can have an adventure on your plate by loading up on all sorts of colorful veggies. When you have a rainbow on your plate, you are getting a full array of vitamins, minerals and other nutri-ents. Plus colorful sides just make everything look so pretty.

- Chili Lime Corn on the Cob
- Brussels Sprouts Amandine
- Cider Mashed Chipotle Sweet Potatoes
- Irish Colcannon
- Mediterranean Kale and Quinoa Pilaf

- Curried Chickpea and Quinoa Pilaf with Cashews and Raisins
- Roasted Lemony Cauliflower and Broccoli with Toasted Pine Nuts
- Chili Spiced Zucchini
- Super Smashed Potatoes
- Dilled Red Bliss Potatoes
- Garden Harvest Ratatouille
- Creamy Butter Beans
- Easy Peasy Polenta
- Spiced Pepitas
- Creamy Asparagus and Leek Risotto
- Curried Butternut Squash Risotto
- Green Bean Mallum
- Sauteed Broccoli Rabe with Cannelini Beans
- Scalloped Potatoes

Chili Lime Corn on the Cob

(serves 2)

Perfect for a summer picnic, these make a tasty accompaniment to Barbecue Tofu and Dilled Red Bliss Potatoes.

Ingredients
2 ears of corn, peeled, cleaned and cut in half
2 Tbl vegan margarine
1 Tbl nutritional yeast
1 tsp chili powder
1/2 tsp sea salt
1 Tbl fresh lime juice

Place corn cobs in pot of boiling water for 3-5 minutes. Meanwhile, in a large bowl stir together vegan margarine, nutritional yeast, chili powder, sea salt and lime juice. Remove cooked corn cobs and place in bowl, turning thoroughly to coat.

Brussels Sprouts Amandine

(serves 2-4)

If you're looking for something a little different to make with your Brussels sprouts, this recipe is it. But feel free to substitute the more traditional green beans when they're in season.

<u>Ingredients</u>
2 cups Brussels Sprouts, stem ends trimmed, outer leaves removed, and cut in half
1 shallot, sliced thin
2 Tbl slivered almonds
1-2 Tbl olive oil
pinch of sea salt

Bring a large pot of water to boil. Add Brussels sprouts and let blanch for 2-3 minutes, or until fork tender. Drain Brussels sprouts into a colander and immediately rinse with cold water. Meanwhile, in a skillet on medium heat, sauté shallot in olive oil until golden. Add slivered almonds and a pinch of sea salt and sauté about a minute more. Add blanched Brussels sprouts and toss together for 2-3 minutes or until warmed through.

Mediterranean Kale and Quinoa Pilaf

(serves 2-4)

This recipe is super simple and it tastes great warm as well as eaten the next day as a cold salad. I like to serve it with Chickpea Croquettes topped with a dollop of Creamy Dill Tartar Sauce.

<u>Ingredients</u>
1 bunch lacinato kale (approx. 10-12 oz), blanched and chopped
1-2 Tbs olive oil
1/2 cup diced shallot
2-3 cloves garlic, minced (to taste)
8 sun-dried tomatoes, cut into strips
1/2 cup kalamata olives, sliced in half
1/4 cup toasted pine nuts
2 cups cooked quinoa
1/4 cup water
approx. 1/2 tsp sea salt (to taste)
1/4 tsp coarsely ground black pepper

Heat the oil in a large, deep pan over medium heat and saute the shallots in the hot oil until soft. Add the garlic and keep sauteing until the shallots begin to turn light golden. Stir in the kale, sun-dried tomatoes, olives, quinoa and water, then cover and reduce heat to low. Simmer for about 5 minutes or until the water has evaporated. Taste for balance and adjust seasonings if desired.

Curried Chickpea and Quinoa Pilaf with Cashews and Raisins

(serves 2-4)

This is a mildly spicy side dish that can be eaten warm or cold, and the flavors come together even better the next day. If you like the balance of sweet and savory with just the raisins, omit the agave.

Ingredients
1 cup quinoa
1 3/4 cups filtered water
1/4 tsp sea salt
1/4 tsp curry powder
1/4 tsp cinnamon
1/8 tsp turmeric
1/4 cup raisins
1-2 green onions, diced
1 clove garlic, minced
1/2 cup chopped cashews
1 15 oz. can chick peas, drained and rinsed
1-2 Tbl agave syrup (optional)

If your quinoa does not come pre-rinsed, place in a fine mesh strainer, rinse, and let drain. Place rinsed quinoa in medium sauce pan and toast on low heat with spices and sea salt, stirring frequently. Add water, cover, and bring to a boil on high heat. Lower heat to simmer for 15 minutes. When all water has been absorbed, fluff gently with a fork and stir in raisins, green onions, garlic, cashews, chick peas, and agave (optional). Season to taste.

Roasted Lemony Cauliflower and Broccoli with Toasted Pine Nuts

(serves 2-4)

Roasting veggies brings out their natural sweetness through the process of caramelization. A squeeze of tart lemon along with savory toasted pine nuts complements the sweetness, creating a full flavor profile that's satisfyingly delicious.

Ingredients

1 head of broccoli (approx. 2 cups), cut into florets
1/2 head of cauliflower (approx. 2 cups), cut into florets
3 Tbl olive oil
6 cloves garlic, peel removed
2 lemons, 1 thinly sliced and one cut in half
salt and pepper
2 Tbl pine nuts

Preheat oven to 475 degrees. In a large bowl, toss broccoli, cauliflower, sliced lemon, and garlic with olive oil, salt and pepper. Spread veggies out evenly on oiled baking sheet(s) and bake for 15-20 minutes, or until fork tender and lightly browned. Remove and discard cooked lemon slices. Meanwhile, toast pine nuts in a dry skillet on medium heat until golden and fragrant. When broccoli and cauliflower are finished cooking, return to bowl and toss with pine nuts and squeeze with 1-2 Tbl fresh lemon juice.

Chili Spiced Zucchini

(serves 2)

It really doesn't get much quicker and easier than this, and yet you'll be surprised at how flavorful this side dish is. Serve with Three Bean Cha Cha Cha Chili and brown rice.

Ingredients
1 large or 2 medium zucchini, cut in half lengthwise, then cut into long wedges
1 Tbl olive oil
1 tsp chili powder
1/2 tsp cumin
1/4 tsp sea salt

Heat a large skillet on medium and add oil when pan is hot. Saute zucchini 3-5 minutes on each side, or until fork tender but still firm. Add chili powder, cumin, and salt in the last minute of cooking and toss to coat.

Super Smashed Potatoes

(serves 2)

These are super because they're super easy and delicious. The secret ingredient is a clove of garlicky goodness.

<u>Ingredients</u>
2 large Russet potatoes, peeled and cubed
1 clove garlic
1/2 cup vanilla rice milk
2 Tbl Earth Balance margarine
salt to taste (approx. 1/2 tsp)

Boil potatoes and garlic 10-15 minutes or until fork tender. Drain and mash potatoes and garlic with rice milk and margarine. Add salt to taste.

Dilled Red Bliss Potatoes

(serves 2-4)
This can be eaten as a warm or cold potato salad. The flavor of fresh dill is a bright contrast to the sharpness of red wine vinegar.

Ingredients
4 medium sized red bliss potatoes
1 shallot, chopped fine
1 Tbl olive oil
1 Tbl vegan margarine
1 Tbl red wine vinegar
1/2 tsp sea salt
fresh black pepper
1/2 cup fresh dill, chopped fine

Bring a large pot of water to a boil and cook potatoes for 10-12 minutes, or until fork tender. Meanwhile, in a large skillet set on medium heat, saute shallot in olive oil until soft, about 3-5 minutes. When potatoes have finished cooking, drain in colander, then transfer to skillet. Stir in vegan margarine, red wine vinegar, sea salt, and crushed black pepper. Taste for seasoning, then remove from heat and gently stir in chopped dill.

Garden Harvest Ratatouille

(serves 4)

Nothing says summer more than garden fresh ratatouille. Although this is a traditional dish, it never gets boring, and I look forward to it every year.

Ingredients
3-4 Tbl olive oil
1 small eggplant, diced small
1 medium zucchini, sliced into quarter moons
1 yellow squash, sliced into quarter moons
1/2 red onion, diced small
2-3 garlic cloves, minced
15 oz. can diced tomatoes (Muir Glen)
1-2 Tbl tomato paste (Bionaturae)
1 handful fresh basil, cut into chiffonade
sea salt and pepper to taste
fresh parsley

Heat a large skillet on medium heat, and when hot add about 1-2 Tbl oil. Add eggplant and a sprinkle of salt, and sauté eggplant for about 5-10 minutes or until beginning to get golden in color. Flip eggplant over and sauté second side for another 5 minutes, or until soft. Remove from skillet and repeat process with zucchini and yellow squash. remove from pan and sauté onion and garlic for about 5 minutes, or until soft. Add tomatoes and cook 5-10 minutes. Combine all vegetables with garlic, onion and tomatoes, then add tomato paste mixed in about ¼ cup water. After sauce thickens, stir in fresh basil, salt and pepper. Garnish with fresh parsley and drizzle of 1-2 Tbl olive oil.

Creamy Butter Beans
(serves 2)

Serve this simple dish as a complement to Garden Harvest Ratatouille. You'll be surprised at how deliciously cheesy and creamy these hearty beans taste.

Ingredients
1-2 Tbl olive oil
1/2 cup red onion, diced fine
1 clove garlic, minced
1 15 oz. can of butter beans, drained and rinsed
1 Tbl fresh parsley
1 tsp dried oregano
1/2 cup water
1/4 tsp sea salt
1-2 Tbl nutritional yeast

In a skillet on medium heat, add oil, onions and garlic, cooking several minutes or until onions are soft. Add the parsley, oregano, water, beans, nutritional yeast, and sea salt and simmer 5-10 minutes or until beans are tender. Stir to prevent sticking.

Easy Peasy Polenta

(serves 6-8)

Polenta is a great alternative to pasta. It can be served as a base for any sauce, as a creamy side for veggies, or cut into squares for appetizers. I like topping little cubes of Polenta with Pumpkin Seed Pesto and Roasted Red Pepper Coulis for a colorful holiday hors d'oeuvres.

<u>Ingredients</u>
6 cups water
2 tsp sea salt
1 3/4 cups yellow cornmeal
3 Tbl vegan margarine

Bring 6 cups of water to a boil in a large saucepan. Add salt and gradually whisk in the cornmeal. Reduce the heat to low and cook until the mixture thickens and the cornmeal is tender, stirring often, for about 15 minutes. Turn off the heat then add the margarine, and stir until melted. Pour into oiled pan and let cool.

Spiced Pepitas

You'll want to eat these as a snack, but they also make a great garnish for Three Sisters Stew or creamy Gingered Butternut Bisque.

Ingredients
1/2 cup pumpkin seeds (pepitas)
1 Tbl vegan margarine
1/4 tsp chili powder
1/4 tsp cinnamon
1/8 tsp sea salt

In a sauté pan, melt margarine over medium heat. Add pumpkin seeds and sauté several minutes until they begin to get toasted. Add spices and sea salt and sauté another minute, or until pumpkin seeds begin to pop. Set aside in a bowl to cool.

EZPZ Tip
Pumpkin seeds are high in zinc, which helps improve mood and minimize Seasonal Affective Disorder, so they're the perfect snack to have on hand in the winter.

Creamy Asparagus and Leek Risotto
(serves 2-4)

I've served this side to nonvegans who can't believe it isn't made with cream or butter. The creamy consistency of Arborio rice makes this a decadent dish, but with very little fat.

Ingredients
1 Tbl olive oil
1 leek, chopped and rinsed well
1 clove garlic, crushed
3/4 cup Arborio rice
1 1/2 cups water
1 cup rice milk
1 Tbl nutritional yeast
1 cup asparagus, blanched, cooled and cut into 1-inch pieces
Sea salt to taste
1 Tbl vegan margarine (optional)

In a large pot, sauté garlic and leek in oil. Add the Arborio rice and sauté for a minute. Add water, nutritional yeast, and about 1/4 tsp sea salt, cover, and bring to a boil. Lower heat and simmer 15 minutes, or until water is absorbed. Remove cover, turn up heat, and gradually stir in rice milk to make smooth and creamy texture. Keep up this process until no more liquid can be absorbed. When you've added enough rice milk, carefully fold in cooked asparagus and season with sea salt. If desired, add a tablespoon of vegan margarine at the end for extra lusciousness.

Curried Butternut Squash Risotto
(serves 2-4)

This is a spicy twist on the traditional risotto recipe. It's delicious served with Green Bean Mallum or simply topped with toasted coconut.

<u>Ingredients</u>
1 Tbl olive oil
1 leek, sliced thin and washed thoroughly
3/4 cup Arborio rice, rinsed in cold water and drained
1 cup butternut squash, peeled and cubed
1 1/2 cups water
approx. 1/2 cup rice milk
1/2 cup coconut milk (Thai Kitchen canned)
1-2 Tbl nutritional yeast
2 tsp curry powder
1 tsp sea salt, or to taste

In a large pot, sauté garlic and leek in oil. Add the Arborio rice and sauté for a minute. Add butternut squash, nutritional yeast, curry powder, sea salt and water, then cover and bring to a boil. Lower heat and simmer 15 minutes or until water has been absorbed. Begin adding rice milk 1/4 cup at a time, gently stirring until the rice has absorbed the liquid. The butternut squash will fall apart as you stir. Keep stirring and adding liquid until creamy, then stir in coconut milk. Season with sea salt as needed.

Green Bean Mallum

(serves 2)

The word mallum means "mix up," and in the case of this recipe, it's a mix of toasted coconut and green beans. Feel free to substitute any firm vegetable of your choice.

<u>Ingredients</u>
2 Tbl shredded, unsweetened coconut
1/8 tsp turmeric
pinch of sea salt
1 Tbl coconut oil
two large handfuls of green beans, trimmed

Bring a large pot of water to a boil and blanch string beans for 3-5 minutes, or until they turn bright green and begin to pop. Drain and rinse in cold water, then set aside. Meanwhile, heat a skillet on medium and add coconut when pan is hot. Stir and heat until fragrant and coconut begins to get golden brown. Add green beans, turmeric, sea salt and coconut oil to the pan and heat until green beans are well coated.

Sauteed Broccoli Rabe with Cannelini Beans

(serves 2)

This traditional Italian side dish of bitter greens pairs well with pasta or polenta. Feel free to go crazy with as much garlic as you'd like.

Ingredients

3 tablespoons olive oil
1 large bunch of broccoli rabe
1/4 teaspoon crushed red pepper flakes
3 cloves garlic, sliced thin
1 16 oz. can cannelini beans, drained and rinsed
1/4 cup tomato paste
2-3 Tbl fresh parsley, chopped
1/2 tsp sea salt
Sea salt and pepper to taste

In a large pot of boiling water, blanch broccoli rabe for 3-5 minutes. Drain and rinse in cold water, then chop into 2-3 inch slices. Heat 2 Tbl olive oil and garlic in a large skillet over medium heat until lightly golden. Toss in broccoli rabe, turning to coat with oil. Season with salt, pepper, and crushed red pepper flakes. Add tomato paste and enough water to make a thin sauce. Cook, stirring occasionally, about 5 minutes. Stir in beans and simmer about 5 minutes. Top with remaining olive oil and chopped parsley, and season with salt and pepper.

Scalloped Potatoes

(serves 2-4)
More creamy goodness in this side dish. Serve it with Easy Peasy Sesame Baked Tofu and Brussels Sprouts Amandine.

Ingredients
2 large Russet potatoes (or 3-4 Yukon Gold potatoes),
peeled and cut into 1/4-inch thick slices
1 cup onions, diced
1 heaping Tbl cornstarch
approx. 1 cup vanilla rice milk
1-2 Tbl nutritional yeast
1/2 cup Daiya mozzarella
salt to taste (approx. 1/2 tsp)

Boil potatoes 10-12 minutes or until fork tender. Drain and set aside. Meanwhile, sauté onions with a pinch of salt in a sauce pot with about 1/4 cup of water. Cook until soft, about 5 minutes. Stir together rice milk, corn starch, nutritional yeast and salt, and heat in pot until sauce thickens. Stir in 1/2 cup Daiya mozzarella until melted and creamy, then add potatoes and let simmer 5-10 minutes on low heat until sauce thickens. Season with sea salt.

Chapter 12

Chorus: Main Dishes

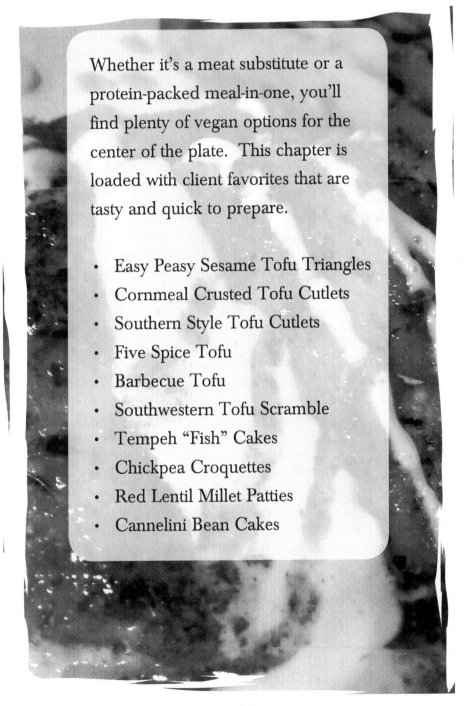

Whether it's a meat substitute or a protein-packed meal-in-one, you'll find plenty of vegan options for the center of the plate. This chapter is loaded with client favorites that are tasty and quick to prepare.

- Easy Peasy Sesame Tofu Triangles
- Cornmeal Crusted Tofu Cutlets
- Southern Style Tofu Cutlets
- Five Spice Tofu
- Barbecue Tofu
- Southwestern Tofu Scramble
- Tempeh "Fish" Cakes
- Chickpea Croquettes
- Red Lentil Millet Patties
- Cannelini Bean Cakes

- Pinto Quinoa Patties
- Spinach, Pumpkin and Chickpea Curry
- Coconut Curry with Tofu and Veggies
- Edamame Succotash
- Jerk Tempeh with Pineapple, Red and Green Peppers
- Black Bean and Brown Rice Stuffed Baked Zucchini Boats
- Italian Mom Approved Walnut "Neatballs"
- Crispy Chewy OMG Good Gluten-free Pizza
- Spiced Pumpkin Seed Socca
- RAW Taco Sliders with Cumin Spiced Walnut Meat
- RAW Manicotti with Macadamia "Rawcotta" and Sun-dried Tomato Marinara

Easy Peasy Sesame Tofu Triangles

(serves 2-4)

This is a versatile recipe that can stand on its own or be modified with the addition of spices such as paprika, chili powder, curry powder or chipotle pepper, depending on the flavor profile you wish to achieve. Play around.

Ingredients
1 lb. extra firm tofu
2-3 Tbl tamari
1-2 tsp toasted sesame oil

Preheat oven to 400 degrees. Drain and rinse tofu, then stand vertically on cutting board. Make one diagonal slice down the center, then turn tofu horizontally and make 5 slices, thus cutting tofu into 12 triangles. In a large bowl, marinate tofu in tamari and sesame oil for at least a half an hour. Place marinated tofu on an oiled baking sheet and bake in a preheated oven at 400 degrees for 10-15 minutes on each side or until golden and firm.

Cornmeal Crusted Tofu Cutlets

(serves 2-4)

A crispy coating enrobes the basic tofu cutlets. Serve this for a holiday gathering with Cremini Mushroom Gravy and Smashed Potatoes.

Marinade Ingredients
1 lb. block of tofu (The Bridge), cut into 8 rectangle slices
2-3 Tbl tamari
1-2 tsp toasted sesame oil

Topping Ingredients
1/2 cup cornmeal
1/2 cup nutritional yeast
1/4 cup corn starch
1 tsp dried oregano
1 tsp chili powder
1/2 tsp sea salt
Fresh black pepper

Cut tofu and marinate in a large bowl for at least half an hour. In a separate bowl, combine topping ingredients. Thoroughly coat each slice of tofu in topping and place on oiled baking sheet. Bake at 400 degrees for 15-20 minutes on each side, or until coating is lightly browned and crisp and tofu is firm.

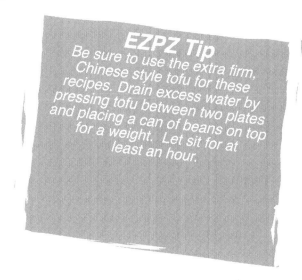

EZPZ Tip

Be sure to use the extra firm, Chinese style tofu for these recipes. Drain excess water by pressing tofu between two plates and placing a can of beans on top for a weight. Let sit for at least an hour.

Southern Style Tofu Cutlets

(serves 2-4)

If you ever have a craving for old school KFC, this recipe will bring you back to your days as a fast food addict. But if you've never had that experience, they're still pretty delicious.

Ingredients
1 lb. extra firm tofu
2 Tbl corn starch
1/4 cup rice milk

Coating Ingredients
1/2 cup nutritional yeast
1 tsp sea salt
1/2 tsp garlic powder
1/2 tsp onion powder
1/2 tsp dried parsley
1/4 tsp paprika
1/4 tsp dried basil
1/4 tsp dried oregano
1/4 tsp curry powder
1/4 tsp dry yellow mustard powder
1 Tbl chili powder

Preheat oven to 400 degrees. Drain and rinse tofu then place block horizontally on cutting board and cut in half width-wise. Slice each half into four 1/4-inch slices, then set aside. In a medium bowl, mix together corn starch and rice milk. In a separate bowl, mix together all remaining ingredients. Dip each slice of tofu into rice milk mixture then into bowl of mixed spices to thoroughly coat. Place all of the coated slices on an oiled baking sheet and bake 15-20 minutes on each side, or until lightly browned and crisp.

Five Spice Tofu

(serves 2-4)

Add a little extra Asian flare to your tofu with this spice mixture. Serve with simple sauteed veggies and brown rice.

<u>Ingredients</u>
1 lb. extra firm tofu
1 Tbl raw tahini
1-2 Tbl tamari
2 tsp toasted sesame oil
2 Tbl agave syrup
1/2 tsp Chinese 5 Spice powder
1-2 tsp water

Preheat oven to 400 degrees. Stand tofu vertically on cutting board. Make one diagonal slice down the center, then turn tofu horizontally and make 5 slices, thus cutting tofu into 12 triangles. In a bowl, blend together all remaining ingredients, gradually adding enough water to make a smooth sauce. Thoroughly coat tofu on both sides and let marinate 30 minutes. Place marinated tofu on an oiled baking sheet and bake in a preheated oven at 400 degrees for 10-15 minutes on each side or until golden and firm.

EZPZ Tip
Substitute tempeh for any of these tofu recipes, but minimize the marinating time to five minutes since tempeh soaks up liquid like a sponge!

Barbecue Tofu

(serves 2-4)
This tofu has the taste of summer. I bake it in the oven, but if you're careful you can cook it out on the grill on a foil lined pan. Serve with Dilled New Potatoes and Chili Lime Corn on the Cob.

Ingredients
1 lb. package of extra firm tofu cut into 8 rectangles
2-3 Tbl tamari
1-2 tsp toasted sesame oil

Barbecue Sauce Ingredients
2 Tbl tomato paste
2 Tbl tamari
1 Tbl yellow mustard
1 Tbl red wine vinegar
1 Tbl agave syrup
1 Tbl olive oil
2 tsp Spanish smoked paprika
1/2 tsp onion powder
1/2 tsp garlic powder
1/8 tsp cayenne
1/2 tsp sea salt
1 tsp corn starch
1/2 cup water

Preheat oven to 400 degrees. Cut and marinate tofu with tamari and toasted sesame oil in a large bowl for at least half an hour. Place marinated tofu on oiled baking sheet and bake 10-15 mins. on each side, or until firm and browned. Meanwhile, mix sauce ingredients together in a small sauce pot until smooth. Simmer on medium heat 5-10 minutes or until thickened. When tofu has finished baking, remove from oven and spoon barbecue sauce over top.

Southwestern Tofu Scramble

(serves 2-4)

This colorful and flavorful recipe works well on a brunch buffet or breakfast any time.

Ingredients
2 Tbl olive oil
1 cup yellow onion, diced
1 clove garlic, crushed
1 red bell pepper, diced
1 green pepper, diced
4 oz. mushrooms, sliced
1 lb. extra firm tofu, patted dry and crumbled
1/2 tsp sea salt
1-2 Tbl nutritional yeast
1 Tbl Dijon mustard
1/2 tsp turmeric
1 Tbl tomato paste

Sauté the onion and garlic in the oil until onion softens. Add the red and green pepper and cook for 5-10 minutes, or until soft. Add the mushrooms and continue to sauté until they become soft. Add the tofu and remaining ingredients and mix well. Continue to cook until water evaporates and tofu is heated through.

Tempeh "Fish" Cakes

(makes 6 cakes)
This is a popular main dish with clients who swear they taste just like the real thing, only better. They're even on the menu at a local diner whose owner twisted my arm for the secret recipe, but now it's not so secret.

<u>Ingredients</u>
8 oz. tempeh, cut into cubes
1 Tbl vegan mayonnaise
1 Tbl lemon juice
1/2 cup very finely chopped green bell pepper
1/4 cup very finely chopped onion
1 tsp garlic powder
1 Tbl dulse powder
1/2 tsp sea salt
1/4 cup corn starch, plus extra for dredging

Place tempeh in pot of water and bring to a boil. Let boil for 5 minutes. Drain in colander and rinse with cool water, then crumble into a large bowl, squeezing out any excess water. Add the vegan mayo, lemon juice, bell pepper, onion, garlic powder, dulse, and salt and mix well. Gradually add the corn starch and mix with your hands to incorporate. Roll mixture into 6 balls, then flatten slightly. Dust each with corn starch. Heat a thin layer of oil in a skillet over medium heat. Fry cakes for 3-4 minutes on one side and flip when golden brown. Fry for 2 minutes on the other side and transfer to a paper towel to drain. Serve garnished with Remoulade and lemon wedges.

Chickpea Croquettes

(makes 6-8 croquettes)

These are reminiscent of falafel, only they're healthier since they aren't deep-fried. The crispy coating comes from a dusting of corn starch.

Ingredients

1-2 Tbl olive oil
1 15 oz. can of chick peas, drained and rinsed
1/3 cup rice flour or chickpea flour
1 tsp toasted sesame oil
1 Tbl tahini
1/4 cup fresh corn (approx. 1 ear)
8 sun-dried tomatoes
1 tsp coriander
1 tsp cumin
1/2 tsp sea salt
2-3 Tbl corn starch (for dusting)

In a food processor, pulse together ingredients until ball forms. The mixture works best if it is slightly dry (you may need to add more flour) and holds together when pressed with your hand. Spoon large golfball sized portion (about 2 Tbl) of mixture into hand and roll into a ball, then flatten into patty. Dust lightly in corn starch, then repeat with remaining mixture until you have about 6 patties. In a large skillet, heat oil on medium and panfry patties for 2-3 minutes on each side. Place onto paper towel-lined plate when done.

Red Lentil Millet Patties

(makes 6-8 patties)
Red lentils cook quickly and meld with the millet as they absorb liquid. Once cooled, they are the perfect texture for forming into patties. Serve these with a simple yellow or green curry sauce.

Ingredients
1/2 cup red lentils
1/2 cup millet
1/2 cup red onion, diced
1 1/4 cups water
1/4 cup green onion
1/2 cup toasted sunflower seeds
1 Tbl tahini
1 tsp garlic powder
1/4 tsp sea salt
1/2 tsp turmeric
1/4 cup corn starch (for dredging)
1/4 cup canola oil (for frying)

Place lentils, millet, and red onion in a medium sauce pot with water, cover, and bring to a boil. Reduce heat to low and simmer 15-20 minutes, or until lentils and millet are soft. Transfer to a large bowl and combine with remaining ingredients except corn starch. Season with additional salt and garlic powder, if desired. Refrigerate until cool, then press mixture together with your hands. You may need to add a little extra water to get the mixture to clump together. Form into 6-8 balls. Flatten balls into 1/2-inch thick patties, lightly coating both sides with corn starch. Coat a large pan with oil and heat on medium. When oil is hot, place patties in pan, leaving space between each. Cook 5-6 minutes on each side, or until lightly brown and crisp.

Cannelini Bean Cakes

(makes 6-8 cakes)
These are a soft and light patty that are nice eaten in a sandwich with roasted red peppers, cashew mayo, and a drizzle of parsley oil.

<u>Ingredients</u>
1/2 cup of quinoa, rinsed
1 cup of water
1/2 tsp sea salt
2 clove garlic, minced
1/2 cup shallots, chopped fine
1 15 oz. can of cannelini beans, drained and rinsed
1/2 cup green pepper, chopped fine
1 Tbl tahini
1 tsp garlic powder
1 tsp dried oregano
1/4 cup brown rice flour
1/2 cup corn starch for dredging
2-3 Tbl olive oil for frying

In a medium sauce pot, combine quinoa, water, sea salt, 1 clove minced garlic and 1/4 cup shallots. Cover, bring to boil, then lower heat and simmer 15 minutes or until quinoa is tender.

Transfer cooked quinoa to bowl with beans, then add green pepper, remaining minced garlic and shallots, tahini, garlic powder, oregano, and rice flour. Stir together, mashing ingredients with spoon as you mix. Add a little water or tahini if mixture does not clump together. When everything has been combined, place bowl in refrigerator to cool for approximately 30 mins.

Remove cooled quinoa mixture from refrigerator and form into patties using a 1/2 cup measuring cup to scoop out equal portions. Flatten to about an inch thick, then lightly dredge in corn starch. Heat a nonstick pan over medium heat and test with a drop of water to be sure it sizzles before adding oil. Then add enough oil to thinly coat bottom of nonstick pan and fry bean cakes on medium heat for 5-10 minutes on each side, or until lightly browned and crisp.

Pinto Quinoa Patties

(makes 6 patties)
Serve these with fresh salsa and slices of creamy avocado.

Ingredients
2 cups rice crisp cereal, divided
15 oz. can pinto beans, drained and rinsed
1/2 cup cooked red quinoa
1/3 cup nutritional yeast
2 tsp onion powder
1/2 tsp cumin
1/2 tsp sea salt
1/4 cup red onion, diced
1/4 cup celery, diced
1/4 cup carrot, grated
1 clove garlic, minced
2 Tbl ketchup
1 Tbl yellow mustard
1 tsp Sriracha

In a food processor, pulse rice crisp cereal into a fine crumb, then set aside. Pulse together remaining ingredients with 1 cup of cereal crumbs until ball begins to form. Place remaining cereal crumbs on a plate. Form mixture into 6 patties and press into cereal crumbs to coat. Line baking sheet with parchment paper and lay patties on top. Refrigerate for 30 minutes prior to baking. Bake at 350 for 20-25 minutes, turn and bake another 20 minutes, or until firm and crisp on the outsides.

Spinach, Pumpkin and Chickpea Curry

(serves 2-4)

This is one of my "go to" recipes when the weather is cold and damp and I just want something to warm my tummy. Fast.

Ingredients

1-2 Tbl olive oil
1 cup onion, diced
1 Tbl fresh ginger, grated
1 Tbl curry powder
1 tsp turmeric
1/2 tsp sea salt
1-2 Tbl tomato paste
1 15 oz. can coconut milk
2 Tbl pumpkin puree
2-3 Tbl lemon juice
1 Russet potato, peeled, cubed, and cooked until fork tender
8 oz. baby spinach
1 15 oz. can chick peas, drained and rinsed

In a large pot, saute onion in olive oil until lightly browned. Stir in ginger, spices, salt, and tomato paste and cook for 1 minute, or until fragrant. Pour coconut milk and pumpkin puree into pot, stir together with spice mixture, and heat until bubbly. Add lemon juice, then season to taste. Add spinach and stir together until leaves have wilted. Finally, add cooked potatoes and chick peas and simmer 5 minutes to blend flavors.

Coconut Curry with Tofu and Veggies

(serves 2-4)

Vary this recipe with whatever veggies you like and serve over aromatic jasmine rice or noodles to soak up the luscious sauce.

Ingredients
1-2 Tbl olive oil
1 cup onion, diced
1 Tbl fresh ginger, grated
2 cloves garlic, minced
1-2 Tbl curry powder
1 tsp turmeric
1/2 tsp sea salt
1-2 Tbl tomato paste
1 15 oz. can coconut milk
2 Tbl pumpkin puree
2-3 Tbl lemon juice
1 yellow squash, sliced into 1/4-inch thick half moons, and blanched
in boiling water until fork tender (about 3-5 minutes)
1 zucchini, sliced into 1/4-inch thick half moons, and blanched
in boiling water until fork tender (about 3-5 minutes)
2 large carrots, sliced into 1/4-inch rounds, and blanched
in boiling water until fork tender (about 3-5 minutes)
1 lb. block of extra firm Chinese style tofu, cut into 1-inch cubes

In a large pot, saute onion in olive oil until lightly browned. Stir in ginger, garlic, and spices and cook for 1 minute or until fragrant, then add tomato paste. Pour coconut milk and pumpkin puree into pot and heat until bubbly. Add lemon juice, then season to taste. Add tofu and simmer on medium low heat for 5-10 minutes, then add cooked veggies and simmer another 5 minutes to blend flavors.

Edamame Succotash

(serves 2-4)

This is a perfect late summer dish when corn is in season and super sweet. If you're not a fan of cherry tomatoes, substitute diced red pepper.

Ingredients

1-2 Tbl olive oil
1/2 cup red onion, diced
1 Tbl garlic, minced
1/2 cup carrot, diced
1 cup frozen or fresh corn, thawed
1 cup frozen shelled edamame, thawed
1 Tbl corn starch
1 cup vanilla rice milk
1-2 Tbl nutritional yeast
1 Tbl Dijon mustard
1/2 tsp sea salt
1 cup cherry tomatoes, sliced in half
1 Tbl chopped fresh parsley
1-2 tsp fresh lemon juice

In a skillet, sauté red onion and carrot in olive oil on medium heat for several minutes, or until soft. Add garlic, fresh corn, and edamame and sauté several minutes more. In a cup, stir corn starch together with rice milk until dissolved. Gradually add to vegetable mixture and stir until sauce thickens. Stir in nutritional yeast, Dijon mustard, and sea salt. Add cherry tomatoes and fresh parsley and let cook about a minute. Lower heat and add fresh lemon juice.

Jerk Tempeh with Pineapple, Red and Green Peppers

(serves 2-4)

If you've never had tempeh, this is the way to do it. The flavors are the perfect combination of savory, spicy and sweet. Pairs well with Caribbean Jasmine Rice Salad.

Marinade Ingredients
1/2 cup yellow onion, chopped
1 scallion, chopped
1 clove garlic
1 tsp minced jalapeño pepper
1-inch piece of fresh ginger
1 Tbl tomato paste
2 Tbl tamari
2 Tbl olive oil
2 Tbl red wine vinegar
2 Tbl agave syrup
1/2 tsp allspice
1/2 tsp coriander

Ingredients
8 oz. of tempeh, cut into 8 triangles
1 Tbl olive oil
1 small yellow onion, cut into half moons
1 red bell pepper, diced
1 green pepper, diced
1 clove garlic, minced
1 cup diced pineapple
1 green onion, diced

Puree all of the marinade ingredients in a blender to form a thick sauce. Coat tempeh triangles evenly and lay on an oiled baking sheet, reserving the remaining marinade. Bake tempeh at 375 degrees for 5-10 minutes, flip and cook another 5-10 minutes until a light brown crust forms.

Meanwhile, in a large skillet, sauté onion in oil until translucent. Add peppers, garlic and pineapple and sauté until soft (about 5-10 minutes). Add remaining marinade and stir to distribute evenly. Pour hot mixture over cooked jerk tempeh and garnish with sliced green onion.

Black Bean and Brown Rice Stuffed Baked Zucchini Boats

(serves 2)

This is a simple and light supper that works any time of the year, but it's best when zucchini is in season. Serve with Roasted Red Pepper Coulis pooled on the side. For added decadence, melt your favorite vegan cheese over the top or drizzle with Chipotle Cashew Aioli.

Stuffing Ingredients

1 cup of water
1/2 cup short grain brown rice
1/2 cup onion, diced
1/2 tsp cumin
1/2 tsp chili powder
1/4 tsp sea salt
fresh black pepper
1 15 oz. can of black beans, drained and rinsed
1/2 cup green onion, sliced

Place rice, water, onion, cumin, chili powder, sea salt and black pepper in a sauce pot, cover and bring to a boil. Lower heat and simmer 15-20 minutes, or until rice is tender. Gently fluff rice and stir in black beans and green onion. Season with sea salt and black pepper.

Baked Zucchini

2 zucchini, sliced in half length-wise
2 Tbl olive oil
sea salt
fresh black pepper

Scrape the seeds out of the zucchini with a spoon, leaving the walls of each hollowed-out half about ½-inch thick. Drizzle with olive oil and sprinkle lightly with salt and pepper. Bake at 400 degrees for about 10-15 minutes, or until fork tender. Fill with black bean and rice stuffing.

Italian Mom Approved Walnut "Neatballs"

(makes about 2 dozen)

Hello spaghetti and meatballs! Even nonvegans will love these traditional favorites. Serve with Fire-roasted Tomato Marinara or Cashew Bechamel. Alternatively, make a double batch and freeze "as is" in a ziplock bag, then pop a few into the microwave for quick heating later.

Ingredients

1 1/2 cups walnuts, toasted
1/4 cup gluten-free panko breadcrumbs (I used Ian's Natural Foods)
1/2 cup brown rice flour
1 tsp dried oregano
1 tsp dried basil
3 Tbl fresh parsley
1/2 cup minced onion
1 Tbl coconut aminos (this takes the place of tamari or soy sauce)

1 Tbl balsamic vinegar
3 cloves garlic
8 oz. cremini mushrooms, chopped
1/4 cup nutritional yeast
1-2 tsp Dijon mustard
1/2 tsp sea salt
1 tsp lemon juice

Preheat oven to 350 degrees. In a large skillet, toast walnuts on medium heat until fragrant. Place walnuts in food processor and pulse until a fine crumb consistency is achieved. Place in large bowl and combine with breadcrumbs, flour, oregano, and basil. Place remaining ingredients in food processor and pulse together until everything is finely chopped and beginning to clump together as the mushrooms and onion release their liquid. Be careful not to over-process into a paste. There should still be some texture to the onions and mushrooms. Combine these ingredients with the walnut mixture and stir together until everything is blended. If mixture is too wet, add a little more flour. Scoop out a heaping tablespoon of the mixture and roll into a ball. This makes roughly 2 dozen, depending on the size. Place meatballs on a foil lined baking sheet coated with oil. Bake for 20-30 minutes or until browned underneath, then flip over and bake another 5-10 minutes. When finished, these will be firm on the outside and tender on the inside. They can be placed in a simmering pot of marinara for 5-10 minutes, just to warm through. Be careful not to simmer too long or they will get mushy and start to fall apart.

Crispy Chewy OMG Good Gluten-free Pizza

(serves 6-8 slices)

When I stopped eating gluten about 10 years ago, the only thing I really missed was pizza. This is my "close to the real thing" crust that satisfies that lingering craving. The key is to cook it in a cast iron skillet for the perfectly crisp bite and chewy texture.

Ingredients
1 package dry yeast
1 1/2 cups warm water
2 Tbl olive oil
1 tsp organic sugar
2 - 2 1/2 cups gluten-free flour
2 tsp xanthan gum
1/4 tsp sea salt

Topping Ingredients
1 zucchini, sliced into thin half moons
1 red onion, sliced into thin half moons
1/2 cup shredded vegan mozzarella
fire-roasted tomato marinara

Preheat oven to 450 degrees and place 10" cast iron skillet in oven while making dough.

Meanwhile, in a large bowl, proof your package of yeast with warm water. Stir in extra virgin olive oil and sugar and wait till it bubbles. Then stir in your dry ingredients, gradually adding flour until dough pulls away from the sides of the bowl and comes together in a loose ball. Carefully remove heated skillet from oven and drizzle with olive oil. Generously dust hands with flour and press dough out into the skillet. Prebake in oven 10 minutes, or until lightly browned.

While crust is in the oven, saute zucchini and red onion in a pan with some olive oil. Remove prebaked crust and top with marinara sauce, sauteed veggies, and vegan mozzarella. Return pizza to oven and bake another ten minutes, or until cheese melts.

Spiced Pumpkin Seed Socca

(makes 6-8 slices)

Socca is a crispy flatbread made from chickpea flour that originated in France. I like it served as a side to a hearty soup or even an Indian curry for a satisfying lunch.

Ingredients
1 cup chickpea flour
1 tsp sea salt
1/2 tsp baking powder
1/2 tsp fresh ground black pepper
1 cup warm water
3 Tbl olive oil, divided
1/2 cup of diced onion
1/4 cup pumpkin seeds
1/4 tsp chili powder
1/4 tsp cinnamon
pinch of cayenne pepper

In a large bowl, whisk together flour, sea salt, baking powder, pepper, warm water, and olive oil. The batter is pretty watery at first and needs to rest in the bowl to thicken, covered with a towel, for at least 30 minutes. Meanwhile, heat a cast iron skillet in a 450 degree preheated oven. In a separate bowl, toss together onion, pumpkin seeds, chili powder, cinnamon and cayenne. When the batter has thickened, take the skillet out of the oven, coat the bottom with about 1 tablespoon of olive oil, and throw in onion mixture and pour batter evenly on top. Bake for about 12-15 minutes, or until lightly browned on sides. Broil for about 2-3 minutes to get some browning on top. Let it sit for a few minutes before cutting into wedges.

RAW Taco Sliders with Cumin Spiced Walnut Meat

(serves 4)

This is a fantastic recipe to eat during the dog days of summer when you're craving spice but don't want to heat up the kitchen. It's quick to prepare and fun to assemble, plus the flavors are sublime. These look lovely in Romaine lettuce leaves for a sophisticated entree, or in endive leaves for a smaller, appetizer sized "slider." Alternatively, they can be assembled on rounds of "zucchini chips" as nachos for a party.

<u>Ingredients</u>
1 cup walnuts, soaked, drained & rinsed
1/4 cup finely diced, sun-dried tomatoes (about 6-8)
1 fresh plum tomato, diced
1 jalapeno pepper, finely diced
1 handful fresh cilantro
2 tsp onion powder
1 tsp garlic powder
2 tsp cumin
1 teaspoon dry coriander
1-2 Tbl lemon juice
1/2 tsp sea salt
8 center leaves of Romaine lettuce, washed and dried

Pulse all ingredients except Romaine lettuce in a food processor until broken down, but still with some texture. Spread about 2-3 Tbl of the mixture in each lettuce leaf. Top with chipotle cashew aioli.

RAW Manicotti with Macadamia "Rawcotta" and Sun-dried Tomato Marinara

(serves 4)
You get all the flavors of "real" manicotti but without all the guilt in this recipe.

"Rawcotta" Ingredients
2 tsp mellow white miso
2 cups macadamia nuts (soaked, drained and rinsed)
3 Tbl lemon juice
1 tsp olive oil
1/2 tsp sea salt
1-2 cloves garlic
1 Tbl onion powder
1/2 tsp dried basil
1/2 tsp dried oregano
Fresh black pepper
2 Tbl fresh parsley
water

In a food processor, pulse together miso, macadamia nuts, lemon juice, olive oil, sea salt, garlic and onion powder until roughly chopped. Gradually add enough water to pulse into a thick paste. Empty half of the mixture into a bowl. Puree remaining mixture with more water to achieve a creamy consistency. Empty into the bowl and stir in remaining ingredients.

Manicotti Ingredients
2 large zucchinis
1 Tbl olive oil
1/4 tsp sea salt

Using a mandolin, slice thin strips of zucchini. Sprinkle with oil and sea salt and set aside to soften. When zucchini becomes pliable like noodles, lay 3 strips of zucchini in an overlapping row to form a rectangle. Spread about 2 Tbl of Rawcotta near one end. Carefully roll that end over the filling and tuck under. Top with marinara.

Sun-dried Tomato Marinara Ingredients

2 ripe tomatoes, chopped
8 sun-dried tomatoes, chopped
8 kalamata olives
1 red bell pepper
1/4 cup extra virgin olive oil
1 cup fresh basil leaves, packed
1 cup fresh parsley, packed
2 cloves garlic
1/2 tsp sea salt
fresh black pepper
pinch of cayenne

In a food processor, pulse ingredients together to combine, keeping some texture. You may need to scrape down the sides with a spatula and continue pulsing.

EZPZ Tip
This recipe can be used to make raw lasagna simply by layering the strips of zucchini with rawcotta and marinara. Alternatively, you can use a spiralizer to make zucchini spaghetti.

Chapter 13

Bridge: Sauces, Gravies & Glazes

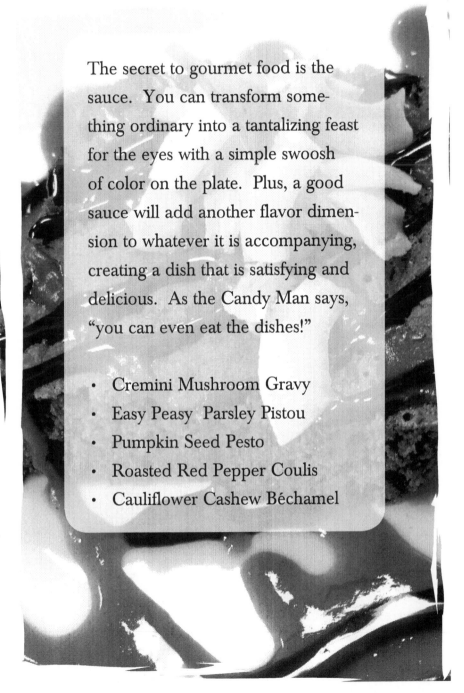

The secret to gourmet food is the sauce. You can transform something ordinary into a tantalizing feast for the eyes with a simple swoosh of color on the plate. Plus, a good sauce will add another flavor dimension to whatever it is accompanying, creating a dish that is satisfying and delicious. As the Candy Man says, "you can even eat the dishes!"

- Cremini Mushroom Gravy
- Easy Peasy Parsley Pistou
- Pumpkin Seed Pesto
- Roasted Red Pepper Coulis
- Cauliflower Cashew Béchamel

- Chipotle Cashew Aioli
- Spicy Horseradish Cashew Sauce
- Creamy Dill Tartar Sauce
- Asian Five Spice Dressing
- Dijon Agave Glaze
- Tahini Lemon Sauce
- Piccata Sauce
- Remoulade
- Spicy Peanut Sesame Sauce
- Fire-roasted Tomato Marinara
- Coconut Cilantro Curry Sauce
- Silken Chocolate Sauce
- Sweet Cashew Maple Creme
- Easy Peasy Raspberry Sauce
- Maple Pumpkin Butter Coulis

Cremini Mushroom Gravy

I make this every year for Thanksgiving to smother whatever faux turkey I happen to be serving.

<u>Ingredients</u>
1-2 Tbl olive oil
8 oz. mushrooms, sliced
1 small shallot, diced
1 Tbl cornstarch
2 Tbl tamari
1 cup water
1 Tbl tahini

In a medium sauce pot on medium heat, sauté mushrooms and shallot in olive oil until soft. Combine cornstarch, tamari and water in a cup. Add to pot and heat until sauce thickens, stirring constantly. Remove from heat and gradually whisk in tahini.

Easy Peasy Parsley Pistou

A pistou is like pesto, but with no nuts or cheese. Drizzle this simple sauce over pasta for a pop of fresh flavor or use it in a squeeze bottle to garnish the plate. It's an easy way to make any meal gourmet.

<u>Ingredients</u>
1 packed cup of fresh flat-leafed parsley, including stems
1-2 cloves garlic
1/4 tsp sea salt
1/2 cup olive oil (approx.)
squeeze of fresh lemon juice

Place all of the ingredients in a food processor and blend until parsley is finely chopped. It should be smooth, yet still retain some texture.

Pumpkin Seed Pesto

This pesto is made without cheese, but the combination of miso, nutritional yeast and lemon give this a cheesy and savory undertone that's reminiscent of the real deal.

Ingredients
1/2 cup raw pumpkin seeds
1/2 cup olive oil
3-4 cloves garlic
1-2 Tbl mellow white miso
1-2 Tbl nutritional yeast
1/4 cup lemon juice
one large bunch fresh basil leaves
one bunch fresh parsley
1/2 tsp sea salt
black pepper

Process all ingredients in a blender or food processor until creamy. If you like a "saucier" pesto, you can add a little water. Add salt and pepper to taste.

Roasted Red Pepper Coulis

This sauce is as beautiful as it is delicious. It pairs well with rice and bean dishes or can even be tossed with pasta.

Ingredients
12 oz. jar of roasted red peppers, drained
2 Tbl olive oil
1 tsp paprika
1/4 tsp cumin
1/4 tsp sea salt
1 tsp apple cider vinegar
pinch cayenne pepper
1-2 Tbl water (as needed)

Puree ingredients in a food processor or blender until thick sauce forms, adding water if necessary.

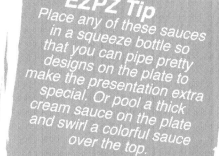

EZPZ Tip
Place any of these sauces in a squeeze bottle so that you can pipe pretty designs on the plate to make the presentation extra special. Or pool a thick cream sauce on the plate and swirl a colorful sauce over the top.

Cauliflower Cashew Béchamel

This rich and luscious sauce tastes decadent, but it has the added benefit of cauliflower hidden in its cream. Serve with veggies and pasta or as a sauce for Walnut "Neatballs."

Ingredients
1 cup cashews (soaked in water at least one hour, drained and rinsed)
1 cup water
1 Tbl lemon juice
2-3 Tbl nutritional yeast
1 tsp sea salt
2 cups of cooked cauliflower (about half a head of cauliflower)
1 5 oz. jar of artichoke hearts
1/2 tsp sea salt
splash of apple cider vinegar

In a large pot of boiling water, cook cauliflower until soft and almost falling apart. Drain and set aside. In a high speed blender, puree cashews and garlic with about 1/2 cup water to bring to a smooth consistency. Add cooked cauliflower and remaining ingredients, then blend with enough water (approx. 1/2 cup) to achieve a creamy consistency. Transfer to sauce pot and simmer on low heat until ready to serve.

Chipotle Cashew Aioli

These sauces share the same base of pureed cashews with variations in seasoning. Feel free to experiment with your own modifications.

Ingredients
1 cup cashews (soaked in water at least one hour, drained and rinsed)
1 tsp chipotle chili powder
1/2 tsp apple cider vinegar
1 Tbl lemon juice
1 tsp sea salt
1/2 cup water

Blend all ingredients in a high-speed blender, gradually adding water to achieve a smooth consistency.

Spicy Horseradish Cashew Sauce

You'll enjoy this poured over Cornmeal Crusted Tofu or as a sandwich spread.

Ingredients
1/2 cup raw cashews (soaked in water at least one hour, drained and rinsed)
1-2 Tbl nutritional yeast
approx. 1/2 cup water
1 clove minced garlic
1-2 Tbl horseradish
2 tsp Dijon mustard
squeeze of lemon juice
sea salt and fresh black pepper

Place soaked cashews, nutritional yeast, garlic and enough water to blend in blender and puree. Gradually add enough water to achieve a thick, creamy consistency. Pour into small bowl and combine with mustard and horseradish. Season with salt and pepper.

Creamy Dill Tartar Sauce

Serve this sauce with Chickpea Croquettes or Tempeh "Fish" Cakes.

Ingredients
1/4 cup cashews (soaked in water at least one hour, drained and rinsed)
1 1/2 Tbl lemon juice
2-3 Tbl water, approx.
1 tsp garlic powder
1/4 cup fresh dill, minced
2 Tbl capers
2 Tbl celery, minced
1 Tbl relish or chopped pickle
1 Tbl red onion, minced
1/2 tsp sea salt

Place cashews in blender with lemon juice and enough water to form a thick, smooth cream. Pour into bowl and stir in remaining ingredients. Mixture should have a slightly chunky texture.

Asian Five Spice Dressing

Use as a sauce on steamed veggies, toss with lettuce, or as a dip for raw veggies.

Ingredients
4 Tbl raw tahini
approx. 1/3 cup water, more or less
2 Tbl tamari
1/2 cup minced scallions
1 clove garlic
2 Tbl olive oil
1-2 tsp toasted sesame oil
2 Tbl agave syrup
1 Tbl grated fresh ginger
1 clove garlic, pressed
1/4 tsp Chinese 5 Spice powder
1/8 tsp ground cumin
pinch of cayenne pepper

In a blender, blend all ingredients until fairly smooth.

EZPZ Tip
Any of these raw sauces can be used as dressings for salads.

Dijon Agave Glaze

This glaze can be drizzled over Easy Peasy Sesame Tofu or fresh steamed veggies.

Ingredients
2 Tbl olive oil
1 Tbl Dijon mustard
1 tsp agave syrup
1/4 tsp sea salt

Stir together all ingredients to create a smooth sauce.

Tahini Lemon Sauce

Another versatile sauce that works well with tofu, tempeh or steamed veggies. It also makes a nice dressing for salads.

Ingredients
2 Tbl olive oil
1 Tbl tahini
1 Tbl Dijon mustard
1 Tbl lemon juice
1 tsp agave syrup
1/4 tsp sea salt

In a small bowl, whisk together olive oil, tahini, mustard, lemon juice, agave, and sea salt.

Piccata Sauce

Serve this with Easy Peasy Sesame Tofu, Smashed Potatoes and steamed asparagus for a simple yet elegant meal.

Ingredients
1-2 Tbl olive oil
1/4 cup chopped shallots
1/4 cup chopped yellow onion
1 cup vanilla rice milk
1 Tbl corn starch
1 Tbl Dijon mustard
1-2 Tbl nutritional yeast
2 Tbl fresh lemon juice
1 Tbl drained capers
2 Tbl vegan margarine
1/2 cup coarsely chopped fresh parsley
1/2 tsp sea salt

In a skillet, saute shallots and onion 1-2 minutes, or until softened. Whisk together rice milk, nutritional yeast, and corn starch, then pour into pan and stir until thickened. Stir in Dijon mustard, lemon juice, capers and sea salt. Just before serving, stir in fresh parsley and margarine.

Remoulade

Serve this as an accompaniment to Tempeh "Fish" Cakes.

Ingredients
1/4 cup vegan mayo
2 tsp Dijon mustard
splash of hot sauce
1 Tbl chopped dill pickle or pickle relish
1 tsp capers
1/8 tsp paprika
1/2 tsp apple cider vinegar
lemon wedges for serving

In a small bowl, mix together all of the above ingredients.

Spicy Peanut Sesame Sauce

This sauce works well with tofu and veggies tossed with rice noodles or over brown rice. Feel free to add some hot chili oil if you like your sauce extra spicy.

Ingredients
3 heaping Tbl creamy peanut butter
6 Tbl water
1-2 Tbl tamari
1 tsp toasted sesame oil
1 clove crushed garlic
1 1/4 inch piece of crushed fresh ginger
2 Tbl lemon juice
1 tsp agave syrup
1/4 tsp crushed red pepper flakes

In a small bowl, mix together peanut butter and water. It will be clumpy at first, but just gradually add more water and stir until creamy consistency is achieved. Add remaining ingredients and stir until smooth.

Fire-Roasted Tomato Marinara

The fire-roasted tomatoes add a depth of flavor to this basic marinara. Use fresh basil when it's in season.

Ingredients
1-2 Tbl olive oil
1 medium onion, diced
3 cloves garlic
2 20 oz. cans of crushed fire-roasted tomatoes
2 tsp dried oregano
2 tsp dried basil
1 tsp sea salt

Saute onions and garlic in olive oil until soft. Add crushed tomatoes, oregano, basil and salt, and simmer on low for 10-15 minutes.

Coconut Cilantro Curry Sauce

Pour this sauce over Red Lentil Millet patties and steamed veggies.

Ingredients
1 cup yellow onion, diced
1 Tbl olive oil
1-2 cloves garlic, minced
2-inch piece of fresh ginger, peeled and minced
1 15 oz. can of coconut milk
1-2 Tbl curry powder
1-2 tsp turmeric
1/2 tsp sea salt (approx.)
2-3 Tbl lemon juice
handful of fresh cilantro

In a medium skillet, saute onion in olive oil until translucent and soft, about 3 minutes. Add garlic and ginger and saute another 1-2 minutes. Stir in curry powder and turmeric. Pour in can of coconut milk and bring to a simmer for 5 minutes. Stir in lemon juice and cilantro, then season with sea salt.

Silken Chocolate Sauce

This is a rich and decadent sauce you will love drizzled over ice cream or your favorite dessert.

Ingredients
3/4 cup cocoa powder, sifted
1/2 cup organic sugar
1/4 tsp sea salt
1/4 cup water
1/4 cup maple syrup
1/2 tsp apple cider vinegar
1 Tbl vanilla extract

In a medium saucepan, stir together cocoa powder, sugar and sea salt. Add water, maple syrup, and vinegar and stir with a wire whisk until smooth. Place over medium-low heat and stir until mixture comes to a low boil. Simmer 5-10 minutes, remove from heat, then add vanilla. Cool slightly before servings on top of dessert.

Sweet Cashew Maple Creme

Put this sauce in a squeeze bottle and use it to garnish muffins or cake.

Ingredients
1/2 cup raw cashews (soaked, drained and rinsed)
1/4 cup water, plus more if necessary
1 tsp fresh lime juice
2 Tbl maple syrup
pinch of sea salt

Puree ingredients in a blender until smooth and creamy, adding more water to thin if necessary. Pour cream into a squeeze bottle and drizzle over dessert.

Easy Peasy Raspberry Sauce

Spread a pool of this sauce on the plate before adding your dessert. Pairs well with chocolate of any kind. I love it with Chocolate Chocolate Chip Brownies and fresh berries.

Ingredients
1 10 oz. jar of raspberry preserves
1 Tbl maple syrup
1 Tbl water

Blend all of the above ingredients together in a high-speed blender until smooth and slightly foamy. Pour into squeeze bottle and squeeze sauce onto dessert.

Maple Pumpkin Butter Coulis

Another simple and flavorful sauce to drizzle on the plate for a pretty and festive flare.

Ingredients
3 Tbl canned pumpkin puree
3 Tbl maple syrup
1/8 tsp sea salt
1/8 tsp cinnamon

Stir together all of the above ingredients until smooth, adding more maple syrup as necessary. Pour into squeeze bottle and pipe onto dessert.

Chapter 14

Coda: Desserts & Sweet Treats

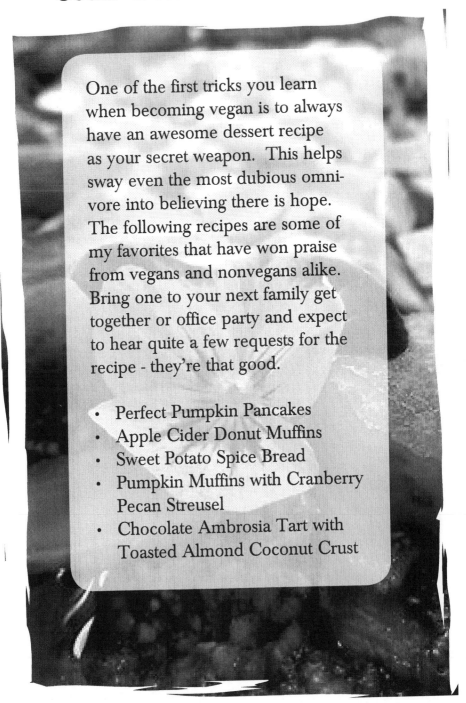

One of the first tricks you learn when becoming vegan is to always have an awesome dessert recipe as your secret weapon. This helps sway even the most dubious omnivore into believing there is hope. The following recipes are some of my favorites that have won praise from vegans and nonvegans alike. Bring one to your next family get together or office party and expect to hear quite a few requests for the recipe - they're that good.

- Perfect Pumpkin Pancakes
- Apple Cider Donut Muffins
- Sweet Potato Spice Bread
- Pumpkin Muffins with Cranberry Pecan Streusel
- Chocolate Ambrosia Tart with Toasted Almond Coconut Crust

- Butternut Mousse with Pecan Praline
- Grandma's Lithuanian Apple Cake
- Chocolate Peanut Butter Cupcakes
- Peanut Butter Chocolate Chip Cookies
- Chocolate Chocolate Chip Brownies
- Pumpkin Spice Chocolate Chip Bars
- Strawberry Shortcake
- Chocolate Lava Cake
- Strawberry Rhubarb Hemp Crisp
- Gooey Toffee Apple Crisp
- Coconut Creme Tapioca
- Cobbler in a Cup
- RAW "Elvis Special" Banana Chocolate Peanut Butter Mousse Tart
- RAW Blueberry Tartlets with Vanilla Citrus Creme
- RAW Coconut Manna and Hempseed Cacao Truffles

Perfect Pumpkin Pancakes

(makes 9 pancakes)
This is my Sunday morning treat, especially after shoveling snow.

Ingredients
1 cup all-purpose gluten-free flour
1/4 tsp xanthan gum
2 tsp baking powder
1/2 tsp sea salt
1/2 tsp cinnamon
1 cup rice milk (room temperature)
2 Tbl agave syrup
1 tsp vanilla
1 Tbl coconut oil, melted

Mix together all the dry ingredients in a large bowl. Whisk together the rice milk, agave syrup, vanilla, and oil, then whisk into the dry ingredients. Stir well to combine. You may need to add a few tablespoons of water to achieve the right consistency. Let sit about 5 minutes while you heat your skillet on medium heat. Add about 1 Tbl coconut oil. When melted and pan is hot, pour about 1/4 cup of batter onto pan for each pancake. Cook 2-3 minutes on first side, then flip when top is bubbly, beginning to dry, and edges underneath are golden brown. Cook another 1-2 minutes on second side.

Apple Cider Donut Muffins

(makes one dozen)
Is it a donut? Is it a muffin? Well, let's just say it's the best of both worlds.

<u>Ingredients</u>
1/3 cup melted coconut oil
1 cup vegan sugar
3/4 cup white rice flour
1/3 cup sorghum flour
1/2 cup tapioca starch
1/4 cup corn starch
1 1/2 tsp baking powder
1/2 tsp xanthan gum
1/2 tsp sea salt
1/8 tsp baking soda
6 Tbl unsweetened applesauce
1/4 tsp vanilla extract
1/2 cup hot apple cider
1 apple, cut into 12 thin slices

Preheat the oven to 350 degrees. Line muffin tins with muffin papers and set aside. In a medium bowl, whisk together the sugar, both flours, tapioca starch, corn starch, baking powder, xanthan gum, salt, and baking soda. Melt the coconut oil with the hot apple cider, and combine with applesauce and vanilla. Add to dry ingredients and mix with a rubber spatula just to combine. Using a tablespoon, fill each muffin cup about halfway, spreading the batter evenly. Place an apple slice in the middle of each muffin. Bake for 15-20 minutes, or until firm and golden. Let cool in the muffin tin for 5 minutes and sprinkle with toppings such as cinnamon sugar or icing, then remove to a cooling rack.

Sweet Potato Spice Bread

(makes one loaf)
This bread is like a dense, moist cake with a touch of warming spice.
It's perfect for cold weather get togethers and served with Chai tea.

<u>Ingredients</u>
1 cup garbanzo bean flour
1/2 cup white rice flour
1/4 cup tapioca flour
1 cup vegan sugar
1 tsp baking soda
1/2 tsp baking powder
1/2 tsp xanthan gum
1/2 tsp salt
1 tsp cinnamon
1/2 tsp allspice
1/2 tsp cloves
1 cup canned sweet potato puree
1/2 cup canola oil
3 Tbl maple syrup
3 Tbl water
1/2 cup chopped walnuts or pecans

Preheat oven to 350°F. In a large bowl, mix together flours, sugar, baking soda, baking powder, xanthan gum, salt, and spices. In a small bowl, whisk together sweet potato puree, oil, syrup, and water. Add wet mixture to dry; combine until just moistened. (Batter will be very thick; don't worry.) Fold in nuts. Pour into oiled loaf pan and bake for 40-50 minutes or until top is browned and a toothpick inserted in the center comes out clean. Let cool 20 minutes; use a butter knife to gently loosen bread from sides of pan, then invert onto a cooling rack. Yields 1 loaf.

Pumpkin Muffins with Cranberry Pecan Streusel

(makes one dozen)

I love the pumpkin cranberry combination and the decadent crunch of crumbly streusel that puts these muffins over the top.

Ingredients

1 cup pumpkin puree
1 Tbl ground flax seed mixed with 3 Tbl water
1/3 cup sugar
1/3 cup brown sugar
1 tablespoon molasses
1 teaspoon vanilla
1/4 cup canola oil
1/4 cup applesauce
1/4 cup water
1/2 cup tapioca starch
1/2 cup rice flour
1/3 cup gluten-free flour
3/4 teaspoon xanthan gum
1/2 teaspoon sea salt
2 teaspoons baking powder
1 teaspoon baking soda
1 tsp cinnamon
1/4 tsp allspice
1/4 tsp cloves
1/4 tsp nutmeg

Streusel Ingredients

In a food processor, pulse together until crumbly yet still chunky:
1/2 cup pecans
1/2 cup dried cranberries
2 Tbl brown sugar
2 Tbl rice flour
1 Tbl vegan margarine
pinch of sea salt

Preheat oven to 350°F. Line a 12-cup muffin tin with paper muffin cups. In a large bowl, whisk together pumpkin puree, flax seed mixture, sugars, molasses, vanilla, oil, and applesauce. In a separate bowl, sift together flours, xanthan gum, salt, baking powder, baking soda, and spices. Combine the two and gradually add enough water (about ¼ cup) to make the batter pourable, yet still thick. Scoop batter with ¼ measuring cup into muffin cups, filling them ¾ of the way full. Sprinkle streusel on top of each. Bake 20-25 minutes, or until muffins are springy, yet firm. Remove from oven and allow to cool in pan only a few minutes; remove to a wire rack to finish cooling.

Chocolate Ambrosia Tart with Toasted Almond Coconut Crust

(serves 6-8)

I've heard "heavenly" to describe this winning combination. It's as pretty as it is decadent.

Crust Ingredients
1 cup almonds
3/4 cup dried shredded coconut
3/4 cup rice flour
2 Tbl coconut oil
1/4 cup agave syrup
1 pinch of sea salt

Filling Ingredients
1 12-oz. package of extra firm Mori Nu silken tofu
1/4 cup canned coconut milk
1/3 cup maple syrup
1 cup of gluten-free vegan chocolate chips
1 tsp vanilla

Preheat oven to 350 degrees. Oil bottom and sides of a 9-inch tart pan. Line with a circle of parchment paper and oil parchment. Place tart pan on baking sheet.

Pulse coconut in food processor to form "flour," then set aside. Pulse nuts, flour and a pinch of salt in food processor. Add coconut flour, coconut oil and syrup and pulse until a ball forms. Transfer dough to tart pan and carefully spread evenly, making sure to press it into the fluted sides. Sides should be slightly thicker than bottom. Lightly prick holes into bottom with a fork and refrigerate for at least 15 minutes. Bake 15-25 minutes or until crust is golden brown and firm. Check after 15 minutes and cover with aluminum foil if sides are browned and center is still soft. Remove from oven and set aside to cool.

Puree tofu, coconut milk and maple syrup in a blender until smooth. Combine with chocolate chips in a sauce pot and heat on low until melted. Stir in vanilla. Pour into cooled crust and chill at least 1 hour. Garnish with fresh berries.

Butternut Mousse with Pecan Praline
(serves 4-6)
This dessert is a Thanksgiving must have.

Mousse Ingredients
1 large butternut squash, cooked
1 cup cashews, soaked in water one hour, drained, and rinsed
1/2 cup water
1/2 cup maple syrup
2 tsp vanilla
1/2 tsp cinnamon
1/4 tsp allspice
1/2 tsp dried ginger
1/8 tsp sea salt

Praline Ingredients
1/2 cup chopped pecans
2 Tbl vegan margarine
1/4 cup maple syrup
pinch of sea salt

To cook squash: Cut in half lengthwise and remove seeds. Place cut side down on baking sheet and bake in 400 degree preheated oven for 20-30 minutes, or until soft. Remove from oven, let cool, then remove flesh from squash and transfer to food processor.

Puree all of the mousse ingredients until smooth and creamy. Chill for at least a half an hour. Just before serving, heat pecans, margarine and maple syrup in a pot on medium heat until bubbly. Immediately pour over the top of mousse, sprinkle with a pinch of sea salt, and serve while warm.

Grandma's Lithuanian Apple Cake

(makes 18 pieces)

This dessert is like a childhood memory for me. My grandmother never wrote her recipe down, but I remember her coring and cutting apple after apple after apple from the big tree in her back yard. I played with this until I got just the right consistency. It's super moist and dense. You'll think there are too many apples, but once they cook down it'll all turn out ok.

Ingredients
1 1/2 cups all-purpose gluten-free flour
1/2 cup brown rice flour
1/2 tsp xanthan gum
1 tsp baking soda
1 tsp cinnamon
1 tsp sea salt
1 1/2 cups Sucanat (unrefined cane syrup)
3 Tbl ground flax seeds, plus 1/3 cup water
1/4 cup coconut oil, melted
1/4 cup apple sauce
1/2 cup apple cider
1 tsp vanilla
3 cups peeled and sliced apples
1/2 cup chopped walnuts

Preheat oven to 375 degrees. In a large mixing bowl, sift together flour, xanthan gum, baking soda, cinnamon and salt. In a separate bowl, mix together Sucanat, flax seed mixture, oil, apple sauce, cider and vanilla. Combine wet and dry ingredients and stir until smooth. Stir in apples and walnuts. Spread batter into oiled 9x13 pan and bake 40-50 minutes, or until edges are lightly browned and toothpick comes out clean. Let cook, then top with powdered sugar if desired.

Chocolate Peanut Butter Cupcakes

(makes one dozen)

This is my "go to" chocolate cake recipe. It's decadent and versatile and can be served with maple creme frosting, raspberry coulis, or pumpkin butter sauce.

Ingredients

1 1/2 cups all-purpose gluten-free flour
1 cup vegan sugar
4 Tbl cocoa powder
1/2 tsp xanthan gum
1 tsp baking soda
1/2 tsp sea salt
1 1/4 cups water
1/4 cup applesauce
1/4 cup canola oil
1 Tbl vinegar
1 tsp vanilla

Preheat oven to 350 degrees. Sift dry ingredients together in a large bowl. In a separate bowl, combine wet ingredients. Pour wet ingredients into dry ingredients and stir until there are no lumps. Pour batter into a muffin tin lined with muffin cups. Bake for 12-18 minutes.

Peanut Butter Frosting Ingredients

1/2 cup confectioners' sugar
1/2 cup creamy peanut butter, natural or organic
4 Tbl vegan margarine
1/2 tsp vanilla extract
1/8 tsp sea salt

Place the peanut butter, vegan margarine, vanilla, and sea salt in a mixing bowl and with an electric mixer, beat until creamy. Add the confectioners' sugar, beat some more, scraping down the bowl with a rubber spatula as you work.

Peanut Butter Chocolate Chip Cookies

(makes 2 dozen)
Continuing with the chocolate peanut butter theme, these cookies are as good as the one's we grew up with as kids. Buttery, smooth, chewy and crisp, they hit all the right spots.

Ingredients
1/2 cup vegan margarine
1/2 cup peanut butter
1 tsp vanilla
2 Tbl maple syrup
1 cup vegan sugar
1/2 cup sorgum flour
1/2 cup all-purpose gluten-free flour
1/4 tsp xanthan gum
1/2 tsp baking powder
1/4 tsp sea salt
1 cup vegan chocolate chips

Preheat oven to 350 degrees. In a food processor, cream together margarine, peanut butter, vanilla, maple syrup, and sugar. Sift together dry ingredients in a bowl, then add to creamed margarine mixture. Pulse in food processor until ball begins to form, scraping down sides with spatula as needed. Transfer batter to bowl and fold in chocolate chips. Spoon rounded tablespoons of batter onto oiled cookie sheet and slightly flatten with your fingers. These will spread slightly when baking, so leave space between them. Bake for 10-12 minutes, or until lightly golden around the edges. Remove from oven, gently slide spatula underneath each cookie to loosen, and let cool on pan 5 minutes before removing. This step is very important because cookies are delicate and crumbly when they first come out of the oven. After 5 minutes, transfer to a cooling rack and let cool completely.

Chocolate Chocolate Chip Brownies

(makes 9)

Everybody loves chocolate, and these brownies deliver that traditional ooey gooey moist texture and rich chocolate flavor that everyone expects from a decadent dessert, but without the refined flour, eggs and butter. They're the perfect treat to bring to holiday get togethers because no one would expect they're vegan and gluten-free. Dress them up with some seasonal garnishes, layer them with fresh fruit for an elegant parfait, or top them with a big dollop of coconut milk ice cream and your guests will be impressed.

Ingredients

1/4 cup coconut oil
1 cup semisweet vegan chocolate chips, divided
2 Tbl ground flax seed + 6 Tbl water (egg replacer)
3/4 cup vegan sugar
1 tsp vanilla extract
1 cup all-purpose gluten-free flour
1 tsp baking powder
1/4 tsp xanthan gum
2 Tbl cocoa powder
1/4 tsp sea salt
1/4 cup water (approx.)

Preheat oven to 350 degrees and lightly oil an 8"x8" pan. In a small sauce pot over medium heat, combine 1/4 cup oil plus 1/2 cup vegan chocolate chips, stirring until melted. Remove from heat and set aside. Place flaxseed mixture in a large bowl. Add sugar and vanilla and blend well. Str in melted chocolate mixture. Stir in the flour, baking powder, xanthan gum, salt, and cocoa powder and enough water to form a smooth batter. Fold in remaining chocolate chips, then pour into prepared pan. Bake approximately 20-25 minutes, or until top is firm. Let cool before cutting into squares.

Pumpkin Spice Chocolate Chip Bars
(makes 9)

These start as innocent blondies, but then they get crazy with the addition of pumpkin and chocolate chips. Feel free to modify to your tastes by adding chopped walnuts or pressing toasted coconut onto the top.

Ingredients
1 cup white rice flour
3/4 cup Gluten-free flour
1/4 cup corn starch
1/8 tsp xanthan gum
1 tsp baking powder
1/4 tsp baking soda
1/4 tsp sea salt
1/2 tsp cinnamon
3/4 cup vegan margarine
1 Tbl coconut oil
1 1/4 cup Sucanat
4 oz. apple sauce + 1 tsp corn starch
1/4 cup pumpkin puree
1 tsp vanilla
2-3 Tbl soy milk
1/2 cup vegan chocolate chips

Preheat oven to 350 degrees. Coat a 9 x 13 pan with oil, then line with parchment paper. In a large bowl, stir together dry ingredients. In a food processor, puree vegan margarine, coconut oil, Sucanat, applesauce & corn starch mixture, pumpkin puree and vanilla until creamy. Add to dry ingredients and stir until batter is smooth. You may need to add a few tablespoons of soy milk if it is too dry. Gently fold in chocolate chips, then spread batter evenly in baking pan. Bake 20-30 minutes or until firm to the touch and lightly golden on the sides. Top with confectioner's sugar.

Strawberry Shortcake with Tapioca Cream

This is a versatile dessert that's perfect for summer picnics when local berries are in season. The cake is moist and tender, but not too sweet. It can be eaten on its own like a muffin, cut in half and served with the low-fat vegan tapioca, or layered in pretty glasses with berries and tapioca cream for an elegant parfait. Whatever way you choose to serve it, the end result is sure to please.

<u>Ingredients</u>
1 1/2 cups almond milk mixed with 1 Tbl apple cider vinegar
2 cups all purpose gluten-free flour (Bob's Red Mill)
2 tsp baking powder
1/2 tsp baking soda
1/2 tsp sea salt
1 cup organic coconut palm sugar (or other organic sweetener)
1/2 cup canola oil
1 1/4 tsp vanilla extract

Preheat oven to 350 degrees. Prepare muffin tins with 24 paper liners. Sift together dry ingredients in a large bowl. Add almond milk mixture and oil and whisk until there are no lumps. Fill each muffin cup about 3/4 full. Bake 15-20 minutes, or until light and springy and a toothpick comes out clean. Cool shortcakes and carefully remove from paper liner before serving. Slice in half and top with fresh berries.

Chocolate Lava Cake

As the name implies, some kind of chocolate goodness is gonna erupt in here. You'll think you made a mistake when the watery batter goes into the oven, but fear not. Soon you will have an ooey gooey mass of chocolate that tastes like a hybrid pudding-cake.

<u>Ingredients</u>
1 cup all-purpose gluten-free flour
3/4 cup organic unrefined cane sugar (Sucanat)
2 Tbl cocoa powder
2 tsp baking powder
1/4 tsp sea salt

1/2 cup rice milk
2 tsp melted vegan margarine
3 Tbl maple syrup
1 tsp vanilla

1 cup organic unrefined cane sugar (Sucanat)
1/4 cup cocoa powder
1 3/4 cup hot water

Mix first 5 ingredients together in a bowl. Whisk in next four ingredients. Pour into ungreased 9" x 9" pan. Mix together Sucanat and cocoa powder and sprinkle over top. Pour hot water over the entire surface of the batter – do not stir. Bake at 350 degrees for 30-45 minutes. The top will be firm, but the inside will be soft when done. As the cake cooks, the topping sinks through the cake to form a pudding layer underneath. Serve with fresh berries and raspberry sauce for garnish.

Strawberry Rhubarb Hemp Crisp

When strawberries and rhubarb are in season this is the dessert to make. The combination of sweet and tart will make you smile.

Filling Ingredients
3 cups strawberries, sliced, reserving about 1/2 cup for garnish
1 cup rhubarb, diced into 1-inch pieces (fresh or frozen)
1/2 cup organic coconut sugar or Sucanat
1 tsp vanilla
1/4 tsp cinnamon
2 tsp corn starch
pinch of sea salt

Topping Ingredients
1/2 cup Erewhon Buckwheat Hemp Flakes
1/2 cup almond flour
1/2 cup all purpose gluten-free flour
1 Tbl hemp seeds
1 tsp cinnamon
1/3 cup organic coconut sugar
1/3 cup coconut oil
1/4 tsp sea salt
2 Tbl sliced almonds

Preheat oven to 375 degrees. In an 8"x8" pan, toss together filling ingredients, then set aside. In a food processor, pulse buckwheat hemp flakes, almond flour, gluten-free flour, and hemp seeds several times until flakes are slightly crushed. Add cinnamon, sugar, coconut oil, and sea salt and pulse until they begin to clump together. Sprinkle topping loosely over the filling mixture, leaving spaces around the edges of the pan, then sprinkle with sliced almonds. Cover with foil and place on cookie sheet to catch any drips. Bake for 30-40 minutes or until fruit filling is bubbly, then remove cover and bake an additional 10-15 minutes to crisp the top. Remove and let cool before serving. Garnish with fresh strawberries and edible flowers.

Gooey Toffee Apple Crisp

Feel free to substitute seasonal fruits like peaches or fresh blueberries so you can enjoy this recipe year-round.

Filling Ingredients
4 apples, sliced into 2-inch chunks
2 tsp lemon juice
1 tsp vanilla
1 Tbl maple syrup
1/4 tsp cinnamon
1/8 tsp sea salt

Topping Ingredients
1/2 cup almonds, finely ground
1/2 cup cream of buckwheat (uncooked)
1/4 cup brown rice flour
1 tsp cinnamon
1/3 cup organic sugar
1/3 cup coconut oil
1/8 tsp sea salt
1 Tbl maple syrup

In a large bowl, combine filling ingredients then place into 8"x8" baking dish. In a food processor, grind slivered almonds until finely chopped. Add buckwheat, rice flour, cinnamon, sugar, oil, and sea salt and process until clumps form. Spread topping over the filling, pressing down lightly. Drizzle with maple syrup. Place in preheated 375 degree oven and bake 30-40 minutes, or until bubbly and browned.

Coconut Creme Tapioca

Tapioca is derived from the root of the yucca plant. It is a starch used to thicken liquid when heated, and in this dessert, when combined with almond milk, it makes a rich and creamy pudding. This recipe has zero added fat and is very low in sugar, yet the flavor is lightly sweet, which makes a nice contrast with tart fresh berries.

<u>Ingredients</u>
2 cups vanilla almond milk
1/2 cup Let's Do Organic granulated tapioca
1/8 tsp sea salt
2 Tbl agave syrup
1 tsp vanilla

Place 1 cup of almond milk and granulated tapioca in a sauce pot and let sit for one hour until liquid is absorbed. Add remaining almond milk and sea salt and place on burner set on High heat. Bring to a boil, then immediately lower to a simmer and cook for 15-20 minutes, stirring often until tapioca is completely transparent and sauce is creamy. Remove from heat and stir in agave syrup and vanilla. Place in serving bowl and refrigerate several hours until thickened. Stir before serving to break up any lumps.

Cobbler in a Cup

Your kitchen will smell like you're baking a pie, but this is a simple one-serving dessert that's perfect for when your sweet tooth craving needs to be satisfied in a hurry.

Ingredients
1 peach, cut into eighths sprinkled with 1 Tbl Florida Crystals
vegan sugar and 1/8 tsp cinnamon
1 Tbl rice flour
1 Tbl gluten-free flour
1 Tbl Florida Crystals vegan sugar
1/4 tsp baking powder
1 Tbl coconut oil, melted
pinch of sea salt
1 Tbl vanilla rice milk

Start by slicing a peach into eighths, place in a mug, then sprinkle with a little bit of Florida Crystals and cinnamon. In a small bowl, mix the flour, sugar, baking powder, sea salt, melted coconut oil and enough rice milk to make thick dough.

Drop dough on top of peach mixture. It won't look too pretty at this point, but trust me, you will be amazed. Microwave your mug of peaches and dough for 3-4 minutes, until peaches shrink, and the dough becomes caky.

RAW "Elvis Special" Banana Chocolate Peanut Butter Mousse Tart

Decadent and delicious, this chocolate mousse has no saturated fat or cholesterol. The walnuts in the nut crust are high in Omega-3 oil, which is anti-inflammatory and helps raise HDL and lower LDL cholesterol. Another good source of oil is avocados which are primarily monounsaturated fat – they also have lots of potassium which is beneficial to the heart and helps lower blood pressure.

<u>Crust Ingredients</u>
1 cup walnuts (soaked, rinsed and drained)
1 cup pecans (soaked, rinsed and drained)
1/2 cup Medjool dates
1 Tbl raw agave syrup
1 tsp cinnamon
Pinch of sea salt

Finely chop nuts in a food processor, then add dates, agave syrup, cinnamon and sea salt and pulse until it begins to stick together. Press into pie pan and refrigerate while preparing filling.

<u>Filling Ingredients</u>
1 cup Medjool dates
1/2 cup agave syrup
1 tsp vanilla
2 avocados, mashed
1/2 cup peanut butter
1/4 cup coconut oil
3/4 cup cocoa powder
1/2 cup water (approx.)
2 bananas, sliced into rounds

In a food processor, puree dates, agave and vanilla until smooth. Add avocado, peanut butter, coconut oil, cocoa powder, and water and puree until creamy. Lay sliced bananas on bottom of prepared crust, reserving some for garnish. Spread filling evenly on top and garnish with sliced bananas. Refrigerate one hour before serving.

RAW Blueberry Tartlets with Vanilla Citrus Creme

These hand-formed tarts look pretty and taste incredibly decadent. Form them into hearts for Valentine's Day and substitute fresh raspberries or strawberries.

Ingredients
2 cups fresh blueberries
2 tsp fresh orange juice
1/2 tsp grated orange zest plus extra julienned for garnish
1/4 tsp vanilla extract
2 Tbl agave syrup
1 cup raw almonds, soaked, drained and rinsed
1/2 cup shredded coconut
8 pitted Medjool dates

Combine first 5 ingredients in a bowl, cover and refrigerate. Pulse almonds in a food processor until they finely chopped. Empty into bowl. Pulse dates with 1 tsp water in food processor until well chopped (they will be a little clumpy). Mix with almonds and coconut to form a paste. Divide mixture evenly into 4 round balls. Place each ball between 2 pieces of wax paper and press to form a 4-inch pancake. Turn up edges for the crust. Refrigerate 2 hours. Use a spatula to move crusts to serving plates; fill each with 1/2 cup berries. Top with vanilla cream and julienned orange zest.

Vanilla Cream Ingredients
1 cup macadamia nuts, soaked, drained and rinsed
6 pitted Medjool dates
1 Tbl agave syrup
1 Tbl coconut oil
1 tsp vanilla extract
pinch of sea salt

Soak dates in 1/2 cup of water until very soft (about 5-10 minutes). Drain soak water and set aside. In a blender, puree macadamia nuts, dates, agave syrup, coconut oil, vanilla and sea salt until smooth. Add date water as needed to achieve smooth and creamy consistency.

RAW Coconut Manna and Hempseed Cacao Truffles

(makes 3 dozen)

If you like the taste of rich, dark chocolate, you'll love these treats. Be sure to keep ingredients chilled while mixing.

Ingredients

1/2 cup Coconut Manna, melted
2-3 Tbl coconut oil, melted
3 Tbl agave syrup
6 Medjool dates, pureed in blender with a couple tablespoons of water to make a date paste
1 Tbl vanilla
1 tsp cinnamon
4 rounded Tbl carob powder
4 rounded Tbl cacao powder
1 Tbl. cacao nibs
1 Tbl goji berries, soaked in water to soften
3 Tbl shelled hemp seeds
3 Tbl dried coconut

In small bowl, stir together melted coconut manna, coconut oil, agave syrup, date paste, vanilla and cinnamon. With a flat spatula, stir in carob and cacao powder until smooth, pliable, and shiny like fudge. Next, fold in cacao nibs and goji berries. Form into balls and roll in hemp seeds and coconut.

Chapter 15

"How do I cook without meat, dairy and eggs?"

Substitute

At first the prospect of switching to a vegan diet can feel daunting because it's as if you are giving up more than you are gaining. However, when you consider that the foods you are no longer consuming generally are not needed for optimal health and can also promote disease with their added saturated fat and cholesterol, their acidifying and inflammatory effects on the body, and if non-organic, their residual hormones, antibiotics and other pharmaceuticals, you really don't want to be eating them. What you're gaining in this process of discarding what you don't need is not only physical health, but peace of mind, clarity of conscience, freedom from exploitation, and a deeper emotional connection to the animals. This bonanza is worth far more than the temporary pleasure of one's palate when ingesting a plateful of suffering.

It's easier than one might think to create meals without animal products. The following list serves as basic guidelines to help you with meal planning for breakfast, lunch and dinner, as well as the occasional baked goods and snacks. Rest assured concerned family and friends, we've got you covered.

Meat

- **Tofu** This versatile fermented soybean based product comes in two styles, Chinese and Japanese. The Chinese style is a firmer, "meatier" texture which works well in stir-fry recipes, baked cutlets and scrambles. Its flavor can be enhanced by sitting in flavorful marinades. The Japanese style is smoother and silkier and is often cubed in miso soup. It can also be blended into smoothies and puddings for an extra boost of protein.

- **Tempeh** Another fermented soy product, tempeh has a denser texture than tofu and is also higher in protein content. It can be simply pan-fried in oil with salt and pepper or baked with a sauce. Be careful when using a marinade since tempeh will soak it up like a sponge.

- **Seitan** Made from wheat gluten, the protein of wheat flour, seitan is a high protein meat substitute. It is typically seasoned with soy sauce, garlic and ginger and used in stir-frys and sautes. It can also be sliced and breaded like a meat cutlet.

- **Beans and Legumes** There is a vast array of options here, whether using them in a soup, mixed with a marinara to make a bolognese sauce, blended into a dip or sandwich spread, or mixed into a salad. They're high in fiber and low in calories, so they'll fill you up without fattening you up.

- **Textured Vegetable Protein (TVP)** This dried protein mixture can be hydrated with water and added to chili, sauce or soup to elicit a "ground beef" texture. It's also a great addition to a vegan pot pie filling.

- **Faux Meat** There are so many meat alternatives on the market that provide taste and texture that are so close to the real thing that some people have trouble telling the difference. Whether they're chicken strips, nuggets, sausage, burgers or bacon, clever manufacturers have come up with vegan alternatives for nearly all of these favorites to help wean meat eaters from the animal addiction. See the "Resources" section for a list of products.

Dairy

- **Milk** Rice milk has a naturally sweet flavor and can be found in blends with carob, chocolate and even Rice Nog for the holidays. Oat milk is another grain based dairy alternative. Almond is the most common of the nut milks, but coconut milk and cashew milk are also becoming widely available. Hemp milk is quickly gaining popularity as a dairy alternative because it's a complete protein and high in Omega-3 oil. Quinoa, chia, sunflower and flax seed milks are also available. Soy milk has long been a staple for vegans and it's also popular as a non-dairy creamer for coffee. You can also make your own EZPZ Nut Milk by blending one cup of nuts (soaked in water at least an hour, drained and rinsed) with 4 cups of fresh water, a drizzle of agave syrup and a pinch of sea salt. Strain through a cheesecloth if desired.

- **Yogurt and Sour Cream** You can easily find soy and coconut based nondairy cultured yogurts and smooth and creamy sour cream that are similar in flavor and texture to the traditional dairy versions. These work great in dips or in baked goods.

- **Cheese and Cream Cheese** There used to be a time when the only vegan cheese you could find were blocks of flavorless processed foods that were about as appetizing as sliced wax. We are fortunate today to have nondairy cheeses that melt, stretch, spread and taste so authentic that you won't even miss that other stuff. Try some nut-based varieties of fermented cheese spread on a cracker or crumbled in a salad. You'll find a list of favorites in the Resources section.

- **Ice Cream** There are just as many options here as there are milk alternatives, and you can find flavor combinations that will make Ben & Jerry feel like a high school phase you were going through.

- **Butter** While margarine has long been a butter substitute, it can also be loaded with hydrogenated oil and trans fats which are not good for you. Plus, some margarines include whey or casein from dairy among their ingredients, so be sure to read labels. Earth Balance is a blessing to vegans.

Eggs

- **Commercial Egg Replacers** The Vegg, Beyond Eggs and Ener-G are commercial egg replacers that can be substituted in any baking recipe. They can also be used to make your favorite scramble, frittata or even a crepe. Who knew you could eat like a Parisian aristocrat and still be cruelty free!

- **DIY Egg Replacers** Ground flax seed is an easy substitute for eggs in baking. When mixed with water, it gets a gelatinous consistency that works well as a binder, plus you get the added benefit of extra fiber and Omega-3 oil. 1 Tbl ground flax seed plus 3 Tbl water = 1 egg. Other substitutes that are the equivalent of one egg and can be used in baking include 1/4 cup mashed banana, 1/4 cup applesauce, or 1/4 cup blended silken tofu. If you just need a leavening agent (something to make your baked goods rise), try using 1 tsp vinegar plus 1 Tbl baking soda for one egg.

- **Mayo** Traditional mayonnaise is made with eggs and oil. There are several commercial vegan mayonnaise brands on the market that look just like real mayo and taste fabulous spread on a sandwich or blended into salads. You can also make your own vegan mayo by pureeing 1/4 cup silken tofu with 1 tsp apple cider vinegar, 1 tsp lemon juice, 1 tsp Dijon mustard and a little salt. Alternatively, you can blend 1/2 cup raw cashews with 1/4 water in place of the tofu for a raw cashew mayo.

What about Gluten?

Although some people avoid eating gluten (the protein found in wheat, barley and rye), it is technically vegan and ok to eat if you are not sensitive to it. However, many vegan products on the market today contain highly refined wheat gluten which one should be careful about eating in large quantities because wheat is acidifying to the body and causes inflammation, both of which can create imbalance and lead to a host of health problems. In addition, wheat is mucus forming and can cause sinus congestion, headaches and cold-like symptoms. For these reasons, all of the recipes in this cookbook are gluten-free and perfect for those with celiac disease, gluten sensitivities and wheat allergies. Gluten-free flours made from garbanzo beans, fava beans, potato starch, sorghum, coconut and rice are substituted for wheat flour and combined with either xanthan gum, tapioca starch or corn starch to take the place of gluten and prevent the baked goods from being too crumbly.

Resources

Animal Rescue Organizations
- Best Friends Animal Society, Kanab, UT
  (http://bestfriends.org)
- Catskill Farm Animal Sanctuary, Saugerties, NY
  (http://casanctuary.org)
- Locket's Meadow, Bethany, CT
  (http://locketsmeadow.com)
- Maple Farm Sanctuary, Methuen, MA
  (http://www.maplefarmsanctuary.org)
- Woodstock Farm Animal Sanctuary, Woodstock, NY
  (http://woodstocksanctuary.org)

Basic Vegan Information
- Food Studies Institute
  (http://www.foodstudies.org)
- Veg Web
  (http://www.vegweb.com/vegan101)
- Vegetarian Resource Group
  (http://www.vrg.org/nutshell/vegan.htm)
- Physicians Committee for Responsible Medicine
  (http://www.pcrm.org/health/diets)

Humane Education
- The Compassionate Living Project
  (http://www.compassionatelivingproject.org)
- Institute for Humane Education
  (http://humaneeducation.org)
- Humane Education Advocates Reaching Teachers
  (http://teachhumane.org/heart)

Vegan Nutrition

- Dr. Michael Greger
  (http://nutritionfacts.org)
- Ginny Kisch Messina
  (www.TheVeganRD.com)
- Brenda Davis
  (http://brendadavisrd.com)
- Julieanna Hever
  (www.PlantBasedDietician.com)
- Jack Norris
  (http://jacknorrisrd.com)

Vegan Products and Brands

- Bionaturae
  (www.bionaturae.com) - tomato paste
- Brad's Organic
  (www.bradsorganic.com) - nut butters, tahini
- The Bridge
  (www.bridgetofu.com) - tofu
- Daiya
  (http://us.daiyafoods.com) - vegan cheese and spreads
- Earth Balance
  (http://earthbalancenatural.com) - vegan margarine, spreads, mayo
- Eden Organic
  (www.edenfoods.com) - canned beans
- Follow Your Heart
  (www.followyourheart.com) - Vegenaise vegan mayo, nondairy cheese
- Hampton Creek
  (http://www.hamptoncreek.com/justmayo) - mayo
- Lightlife
  (www.lightlife.com) - tempeh
- Mori Nu
  (www.morinu.com) - silken tofu
- Muir Glen
  (www.muirglen.com) - fire-roasted tomatoes
- Nutiva
  (http://nutiva.com/) - raw hemp seeds, chia seeds, coconut oil
- Pacific Foods
  (www.pacificfoods) - nondairy beverages

- Rice Dream
  (www.tastethedream.com) - nondairy beverages, frozen desserts
- San-J
  (www.san-j.com) - tamari
- So Delicious
  (www.sodeliciousdairyfree.com) - nondairy beverages and frozen desserts
- Thai Kitchen
  (www.thaikitchen.com) - coconut milk, rice noodles
- Tinkyada
  (www.tinkyada.com) - rice pasta
- Turtle Island Foods "Tofurky"
  (www.tofurky.com) - faux meat products
- Westbrae Naturals
  (www.westbrae.com) - canned beans
- Wholesome Sweeteners
  (www.wholesomesweeteners.com) - Sucanat, organic sugar, raw agave syrup

Vegan Restaurant Guides
- Happy Cow
  (http://www.happycow.net)
- Veg Dining
  (http://www.vegdining.com)
- Veg Guide
  (http://www.vegguide.org)

Vegan Shopping
- Alternative Outfitters
  (http://www.alternativeoutfitters.com)
- Herbivore Clothing
  (http://www.herbivoreclothing.com)
- Vegan Chic
  (http://www.veganchic.com)
- Vegan Essentials
  (http://www.veganessentials.com)
- Vegan Store
  (http://www.veganstore.com)
- If Dogs Could Sing
  (www.ifdogscouldsing.com)
  A CD sung from the dog's perspective. Proceeds fund

animal rescue efforts.

Vegan Non-Profit Organizations

- Compassion Over Killing
  (www.cok.net)
- FARM USA
  (www.farmusa.org)
- Mercy for Animals
  (www.mercyforanimals.org)
- North American Vegetarian Society
  (www.navs-online.org)
- Northern Connecticut Vegetarian Society
  (www.northctveg.org)
  Physicians Committee for Responsible Medicine
  (http://pcrm.org)
- Tribe of Heart
  (http://tribeofheart.org)
- Vegan Outreach
  (http://veganoutreach.org)

About the Author

Mary Lawrence is executive chef and owner of Well on Wheels, Connecticut's premier vegan personal chef service which offers whole foods plant-based meals prepared in clients' homes, group cooking classes, corporate wellness workshops, and private cooking and raw food lessons. She is a frequent guest on radio and TV, including WNPR's "The Colin McEnroe Show" and WTNH-TV's  "CT Style," and a speaker at numerous conferences and seminars, including the inaugural Connecticut Vegetarian & Healthy Living Festival (2012).

She is a writer and food blogger, and her culinary creations can be followed on the blog, The Traveling Vegan Chef (http://wellonwheels.blogspot.com). In 2011 she won the VegOnline.org "Vegetarian Website Award for Excellence." She is a contributor to the Friends of Animals' cookbook, *The Best of Vegan Cooking* (2009), and in 2007 she published her first cookbook, *Quick and Easy Vegan Cuisine*. Her most recent cookbook, *Easy Peasy Vegan Eats* (2014), is a guide for people making the vegan transition.

Mary earned a certificate in plant-based nutrition from the Dr. T. Colin Campbell Foundation at eCornell University, an MA in Communication from the University of Hartford and a BA in English from the University of Connecticut. She has been an adjunct professor at Gateway Community College, University of Hartford, and Manchester Community College. She studied culinary arts at the Natural Gourmet Institute in New York City, and has trained in the kitchen of It's Only Natural restaurant in Middletown, CT.

34468327R00108

Made in the USA
Lexington, KY
06 August 2014